Self-Portrait
Poetry Collection

SELF-PORTRAIT
POETRY COLLECTION

Edited by
Melanie Villines

Art by
Odilon Redon

SILVER BIRCH PRESS
LOS ANGELES, CALIFORNIA

© COPYRIGHT 2014, Silver Birch Press, ALL RIGHTS RESERVED

ISBN-13: 978-0692302422

ISBN-10: 0692302425

FIRST EDITION, October 2014

Email: silver@silverbirchpress.com

Web: silverbirchpress.com

Blog: silverbirchpress.wordpress.com

Cover and interior art: Odilon Redon (1840-1916).

Mailing Address:
Silver Birch Press
P.O. Box 29458
Los Angeles, CA 90029

Note: Authors retain all rights to their poems. If you wish to contact one of the poets, send an email to silver@silverbirchpress.com and we will forward the message.

Introduction

Melanie Villines

The word "self-portrait" usually calls to mind a painting by a famous artist such as Vincent van Gogh, Frida Kahlo, or Pablo Picasso. With the advent of smart phones, the word "selfie" has entered the lexicon, and anyone and everyone can create their own portraits—and Instagram allows people to turn the images into works of art. A less known or practiced art is the poetic self-portrait, where the writer creates a study in words of himself or herself. We found the idea of self-portrait poetry fascinating and fun—yet a bit frightening—and to explore the possibilities issued a call for submissions during July 2014.

From August 1-31, 2014, the Silver Birch Press blog (silverbirchpress.wordpress.com) featured self-portrait poems by sixty-seven authors from thirteen countries—Australia, Austria, Canada, Colombia, India, Norway, Pakistan, Russia, Singapore, Sweden, United Arab Emirates, United Kingdom, and the United States (California, Illinois, Kentucky, Massachusetts, Michigan, New Mexico, New York, North Carolina, Ohio, Oregon, Pennsylvania, Texas, Virginia, and Washington).

The poets offered portraits of themselves that were, by turns, humorous, heartfelt, harrowing, honest, stunning, surreal, and full of surprises.

We hope the brave souls who penned these poems will inspire you to take the plunge and write a self-portrait of your own.

Contents

Kathryn Almy / 13

Cynthia Anderson / 15

Ivan Argüelles / 17

Ronald Baatz / 21

Suvojit Banerjee / 25

Carol Berg / 27

Alan Birkelbach / 29

Eric Burke / 33

Ana Maria Caballero / 35

Mary-Marcia Casoly / 37

Tobi Cogswell / 39

Beth Copeland / 43

Anthony Costello / 45

Tasha Cotter / 49

Kaila Davis / 51

Daniel Patrick Delaney / 53

Rodrigo V. Dela Peña, Jr. / 55

David Diaz / 59

Barbara Eknoian / 63

Annette Foley / 67

Jack Foley / 69

Michael Friedman / 73

Jeannine Hall Gailey / 75

Phillip Giambri / 77

John A. Grochalski 79

Clara Hsu / 81

Elizabeth Jacobson / 83

Loukia M. Janavaras / 85

Mathias Jansson / 87

Jax NTP / 89

Kasey Johnson / 91

Jennifer Lynn Krohn / 95

Angela La Voie / 99

Roz Levine / 103

Alexander Limarev / 105

Stephen Linsteadt / 107

Tamara Madison / 109

Adrian Manning / 111

Michael Mark / 113

Daniel McGinn / 115

Victoria McGrath / 117

Bob McNeil / 121

Ann Menebroker / 125

Danielle Mitchell / 127

karla k. morton / 129

Robert Okaji / 131

Jay Passer / 133

Alan Passman / 135

D.A. Pratt / 139

Billy Roberson / 141

Rizwan Saleem / 143

Paul Sands / 145

Rebecca Schumejda / 147

roy anthony shabla / 149

Sheikha A. / 159

Jakia Smith / 163

Kimberly Smith / 165

Eddie Stewart / 167

Jacque Stukowski / 169

Rosa Swartz / 173

Simen Moflag Talleraas / 175

Keyna Thomas / 177

Sarah Thursday / 179

A. Garnett Weiss / 183

Denise R. Weuve / 185

Liz Worth / 189

Birgit Zartl / 191

Notes from the Poets / 193
About the Poets / 197

SELF-PORTRAIT
POETRY COLLECTION

Kathryn Almy

Self-Portrait as Dog with a Mouthful of Feathers

I didn't kill it myself, but I seem to float
towards decay.
       Instinct says stop,
drop and roll whenever any corpse washes up,

sand in my fur, this smell

changing me in a chemical way
not even my ancestors understood.

Fluff and bones are trophies, like snow-
flakes, socks, bumblebees: treasures I bury.

I open my mouth to shout in triumph, but
out comes only a hoarse croak
and puff of sticky, tickling down

       —the blades and barbs are black, mashed,
       the little white eyes hardly show,
       the iridescence dimmed.

It feels like being beaten for crimes I cannot see.

There is a knot within me: feathers, bugs, scum, and bark

       —everything I have eaten,

this eternal world beyond the reach of words.

Cynthia Anderson

Self-Portrait in a Convex Faucet

The shine of chrome forms a mirror,
the essence of surprise, as I lean over the sink
and find myself doubled, with no more substance
than a passing cloud. The woman I see there
has a face intensified by worry and age,
yet a torso that whispers out of time,
miraculously youthful through a trick
of perception. Outside, the low roar
in the pines tells me the wind is up—
a sound I know intimately, like the pounding
of blood in my body, a sound I could listen to
forever, and would, if given the chance—
but, having only the moment, I grab my camera,
hold it over my face, and click.

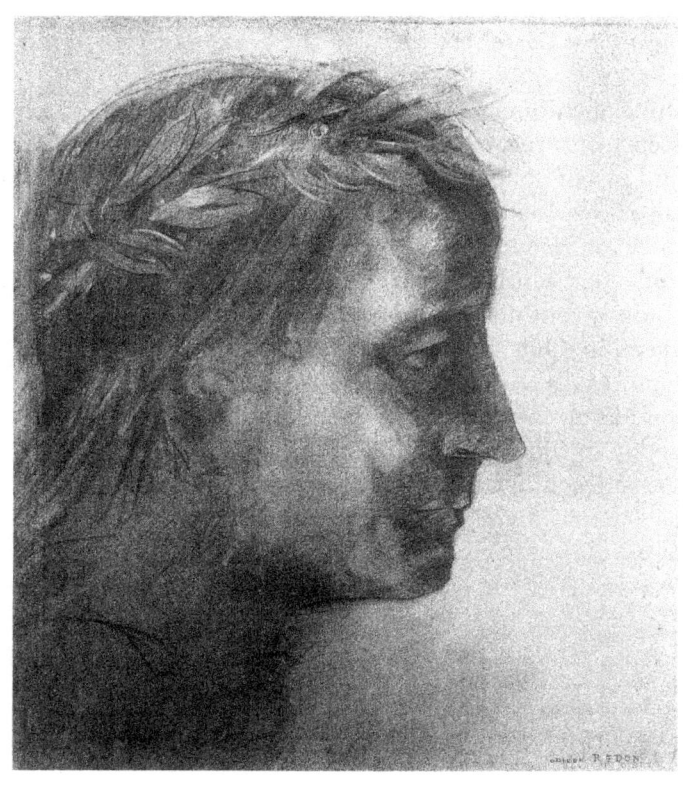

IVAN ARGÜELLES

Orphic Cantos

37.

satellite planets hovering on the rim of thought
white powder in which the dead recognize other souls
this the anti-earth of Persephone the thin lunar crevice
known as salvation for those that succeed in hanging on
a daimon resides in my head pushing sideways into inferno
legacy of ancient poetry untranslatable traces and dreams
of the other life where the elysian fields extend behind the moon
cold cataracts pour into gassy space the relics of the epic
I am if nothing else the stifling afternoon of Sicilian myth
fragments of rock and vegetation dried air volcanic ash
from which arise spectra shuddering from the noon blasts
pleading to have back some shred of shadow a small darkness
a daimon increases his infinite size within my aching brain
there are things my thumbs cannot know to touch that burn
without sensation of flame that contain forbidden metastases
echoes of the first death for those who undergo the second one
when I reemerged from the oracular furnace feet first
my body was radiant this the daimon's irredeemable gift
who filled my mind with the voices of a thousandfold gods
in the lair of heat which is the chrysalis of the omniverse
how can a man ever return who has *seen* and be greeted
by household members as the same when he is polluted
infected by the miasma of being *other* the outsider?

a petty fable jumping from the chariot to earth
the unwholesome goddess inheres to her mortal prey
breath endowing and seizes his limbs in the love act
contractures and stigmata characterize the corporeal domain
perceptions hair-thin of anterior lives vanish in the light
a man this once wandering between stone and rock
mind consumed by the daimon a fierce rippling
fire and ether demand their utter spheres alone
and him leave lost wingless pilgrim without memory
to traverse aimlessly the half familiar terrain
was this his summer once was this the lawn
from which he surveyed by night the starry masses? ➤

do I want out of my head? can I get anything back?
cannot tell the difference between a god and a mortal
the one hides behind a marble statue pretending
to be the statue the other resides inside the marble urn
pretending nothing but the dizzy universe of ash
the daimon inside my head determines the distance
between the two and never tells the truth
entangled in the chronological vertigo of myth

Aphrodite daughter of thought how many are you?
and equally infinite is the number of Cupids
surrounded by their annoying green-winged house flies
swirling inside my poor skull destroying all decorum
so smitten am I ever to escape this amorous infection
or am I destined to revolve between the seven heavens
and the consecutive but numberless floors of Hades?

mythiform worlds crazy ash white disorder the body
simulacrum of the series of deaths rotating in space
just inches from the small aperture inside my mind
where the daimon pushes and pulls and threatens loudly
summer's out the end is here trees all die too green's gone
smashing invisible and immense objects against the air
I am withering vibrating wavering in the middle of sleep
dreaming what is happening here is also happening
on planet Love where all the girls wear Eurydice faces
pale paler than the moon's last thought dissolving
like a mint on the roof of the god's intricate mouth
and which god that is and what name he can possibly have
and just why we are inside him recklessly driving
large polished metal cars through the invention of white
right into the remaining hemisphere of the cranium
the despair of a vowel one too many and the end of time

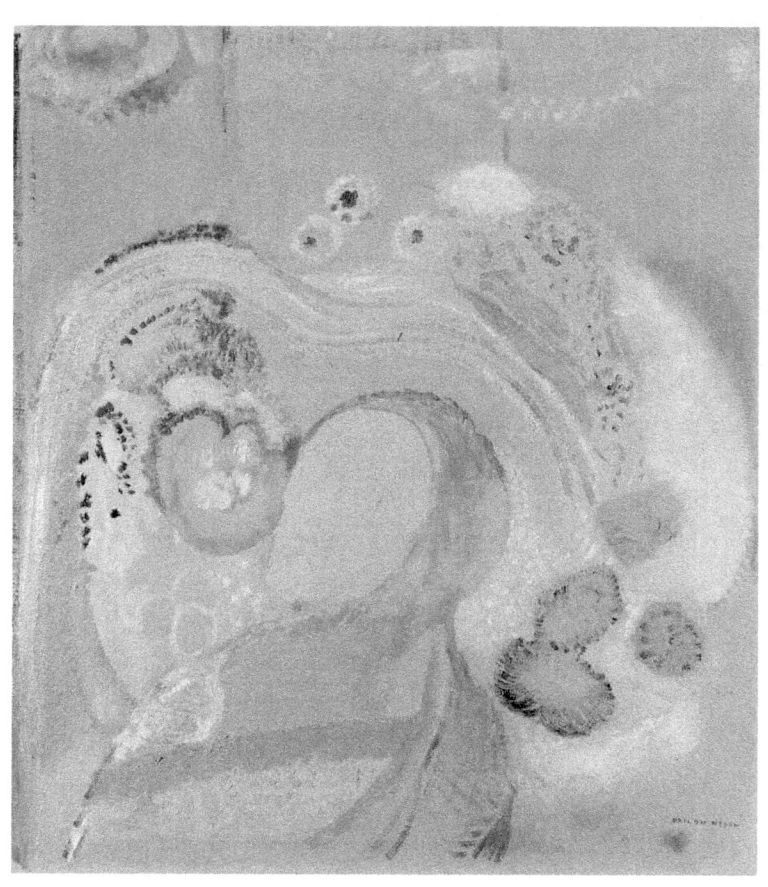

Ronald Baatz

Moving to the Desert

I cannot live here when I am old.
It is too cold for many months out of the year.
As it is, I am having a rough time dealing with

the cold now. When I am old I want to live
in the desert. I suppose this is a common goal
for people who live in the cold. Although, thankfully,

this past winter was a blessing, so unbelievably mild was it.
The morning newspaper explains why
there is such an abundance of yellow jackets.

I was stung recently. I was sitting on the green lawn chair
at the back of the house, minding my own business, reading,
when suddenly I felt an itch on my leg. As I scratched this itch,

one of these yellow jackets let me have it. It had managed to crawl
up my leg, underneath my pants. After stinging me
it fell to the ground and walked away; for some reason not flying,

perhaps too exhausted from having stung me.
My first instinct was to kill it; instead I just moved away from it.
I will leave these heavenly purple mountains to the bugs and the bears

and whatever else wants to claim them as their own.
I do not want to be exposed to such cold when I am old.
I want to bake in the sun. I want to be like a dried fig.

If I had money, then living here would not be such a hardship.
I'd be able to defend myself from the cold with money.
But there is none, and there appears to be nothing I can do

to rectify this problem. I live where the winters are harsh and
I have no way of keeping myself warm. I am profoundly disappointed
in myself. I will not even have the money necessary to move ➤

to the desert when the time comes. So why do I even talk about it,
dream about it. I have been pathetic at creating a decent income.
I will die in this lousy cold. I can see it all now: when I die

others will come to take my body away, my belongings.
They will make a thorough search of my room for money
that I might have hidden away, and they will find not a dime.

Then they will unearth thousands
of poems, and they will know why.

Woodstock, 1985

SUVOJIT BANERJEE

Putting together the pieces of myself

A little boy
wistfully star-gazing on a night, and seeking
warmth from the farthest corners of the
universe; the hapless man
standing amidst the heat-haze
of a city crowded with faces
unknown, and talking
to a cat,
thinking it will lead him to love.
A shy, timid creature
who's Dorian Gray at self-love,
yet knee-weak for that toddler
and its toothless smile.
A romantic who dwells
on the hypocrisies of seeking infinity
in finite, flesh-and-blood
relationships.
Little pieces of stardust
fall from the sky
while stars tinkle, and they become
fireflies.
Tiny droplets of love
trickle down through the mountains
and manifest unto
valleys.
One by one
faces come, faces fade
bucketful of memories,
images in a million mirrors;
They become
me.

Carol Berg

Self Portrait as Wife as House as Housewife

The gold chain wrapped around
your throat menaces me.
The sky is in the basement with
empty beer bottles and discarded baby
seats. You think mice have invaded
but really they're clouds making all that mess
clouds that risk their throats for the steel you've
laid bare. You come in with your tools
and bring me down down the stairs
again to show me. The goats are tied up here
bleating. I want their solace I want
their sturdy hooves. The dryer turns
its unconventional rotation into a study
of wheels of cogs of squeals. I squeeze
the washcloths and soap refuses
to come out to release itself to vacate.
I wish for the vacancies of garages
of cupboards holding the last of the Halloween
candy bars. I try to refuse the bleach you
offer try to refuse your stares.
Your leash singing on the hook.

Alan Birkelbach

Silver Age

The eyes, surrounded by lines, of course, are by Kubert,
as is the day-old beard. It is always a day-old beard.
Even after I shave. Sgt. Rock always had a shadow.
I always have a shadow.

You might think I have no input at all from Gil Kane
but if the light is just right
you'll see the vertical tendon
that goes from my cheekbone to the top of my jaw,
there for no apparent reason.

There's a hint, I'd like to think, from Carmine Infantino
in the little half smile I'm casting, kind of like when
Barry Allen was first starting to date Iris and couldn't let her know
he was actually The Flash.

There, at the base of my neck, you might notice the
lax skin, wrinkled, kind of turtle-like, freckled.
Why do I look so stretched out right there, you might say
and then you will realize that
Berni Wrightson was given the shoulders and neck
and he really likes to add a touch of pending macabre,
full of sinew and age.

My bushy eyebrows are obviously Barry Smith
in his finest Zukala-Conan period. It is a shame
that I cannot conjure demons.

My head is long. Jim Aparo did that.
He's always liked long heads. That and he drew
the little silver in my hair around my temples
like on The Phantom Stranger. ➢

You notice how I am facing the mirror squarely,
emphasizing the shoulders. You can even see the
lines of my breastbone through the t-shirt.
That's because Jack Kirby drew that part of me that way
(although there are times I think someone else
might have done the inking.)

Sadly, there is no part of me that is Steranko,
No false perspectives, no layering of muscles.
And neither is there any part of me that you can see
that is penciled, and penciled only, by Neal Adams.
I stay within the frame. I am not cinematic.

And lastly,
if the mirror was only a little wider
then you would see just off to the side
my concubine, obviously designed by Wally Wood,
her massive bosom perfectly round,
and impossibly full.

Eric Burke

Self-Portrait

As a kid,
he couldn't get enough light

to go through the aperture
from the small mirror.

At forty-two,

he finally sees
rotifers in the bird bath water.

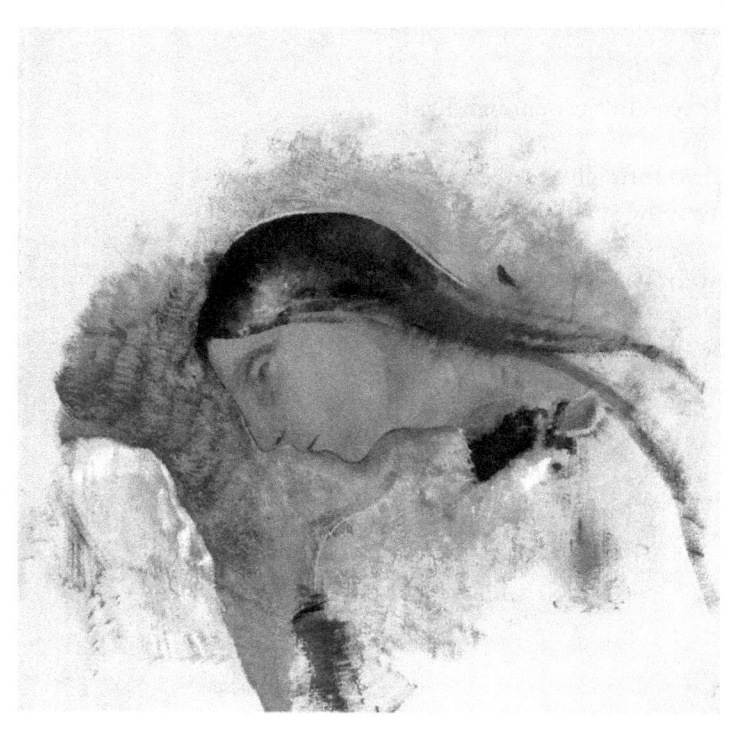

Ana Maria Caballero

Said and Done

I fear my capacity to guide
Mistake toward fulfillment

At times, I blame:

>The flurry of misprint,
>of crisis to unscramble;

>The renewed promise
>of classic self-improvement;

>The flat-water buoyancy
>of fresh peace.

Other times, I blame:

>This devotion
>to words and their construction –

>How they unsay as they say –
>How they commit to purpose as thought –
>How they slay aim through speech –
>How they make me prove and reprove this power –

>This lack.

Mary-Marcia Casoly

Musing on a Self-Portrait

An invisible smile on the world
like the new moon, we are an impostor
and the photograph captures
the whites of my eye:
more hawk than sparrow,
how unsettling, how difficult to read
a blind crow down a well.
A perfect charcoal line smudge the shaft of my nose,
shadows fill our abyss.
There is that one black coarse hair in the thick arc of
eyebrow which begs plucking.
Out of that single eye spills crow's feet
as if my face is her mask formed over with
desire in blackouts or should it be whiteout~
shuttling sorrow from the milky way. The face is extremely cropped.
This unsettling visage~
her head resting upon my hand. My hand holding up
her head. She/Me lay out beneath the mask sky
tonight, learn. What is a meteor?
Do you remember how when we were children, we were chastised
for staring. Don't be vulgar, someone would say across the dining
room table.
Strangeness is a necessary ingredient in beauty
laughs Baudelaire.
For hours make *we* an appearance
all peaked and small waves
—yet it shines, this love, it keeps.
There is no exquisite beauty without some sense of strangeness
in its proportions, quotes Poe
A giant bruise of smeared blue shadow.
The horizon itself must bear so much on its back, like the moon,
like the earth. *Your soul will not want to avoid or neglect regions of your heart*
that do not fit the expected, whispers Poe.

Tobi Cogswell

Self Portrait

She always had some tingling in her hands.
The tips of her left thumb and forefinger were numb,
sometimes her face got tingly and sometimes
she would walk down the hallway at work and
hit the corner of the wall. Numbness and tingling
happened to everyone and it just wasn't that
big a deal. She might have twisted something
or pulled something. Occasionally she couldn't
fasten her necklace but she didn't have that
much jewelry anyway.

One day she had double vision. If she covered
her left eye she saw perfectly. If she covered her
right eye she saw perfectly. If she uncovered
both eyes she saw double. Not like the time
Tommy Jackson sat on her glasses in third grade,
just double.

She called her parents, not to worry them but
to let them know she would be going to the
hospital to find out what was wrong. She covered
one eye, and drove herself.

The doctor was a very nice man. He told her
to "hop up and let's see what's going on." The
room was dimly lit and she worried that
he wouldn't be able to see. She got on the bed
with no blankets or pillows and stared at the
ancient black phone on the bedside table. Somehow
she had changed out of her clothes but couldn't
remember when, she was so scared. ➢

The doctor positioned her perfectly—on her left side,
knees bent, left arm under her head, not knowing
what to expect. Her parents were there but
her mother was so upset she stayed on the other side of
the pale white-blue curtain. Her father stayed to comfort
her mother and there was no one to hold her hand.

The pop of the spinal tap came with excruciating pain.
She would never forget the champagne-cork sound
of the needle puncturing her spine, she could not believe
any human could withstand what was being done to her. And
then the doctor held up a syringe of spinal fluid for her
to see and said "the fluid is clear, you don't have
meningitis" but that was the beginning of her own private hell.

Beth Copeland

Witch

She gazed in the mirror as a young girl
at her rosy, apple-cheeked twin,
staring until her face shifted into
a silver-haired woman's.

A trick of light refracted
from a sheet of mercury glass.
Still, it was a forecast—
the sharp, sunken cheeks

she would someday glimpse,
a woman staring back
in a shop window, a stranger
from another lifetime.

Mirror, mirror

From another lifetime
in a shop window, a stranger,
a woman staring back.
She would someday glimpse

the sharp, sunken cheeks.
Still, it was a forecast
from a sheet of mercury glass,
a trick of light refracted.

A silver-haired woman
staring until her face shifted into
the rosy, apple-cheeked twin
she saw in the mirror as a young girl.

Anthony Costello

Written on the Eve of My 50th birthday
(A slow, meaningful, early morning poem)

after Gregory Corso

I am 49 Years Old.
I look my age. My hair is greying.
There is the emergence of jowls.
Blood vessels map the sides of my nose.
I have always thought my nose big?
My lips have pretty much remained the same.
My eyes always surprise me. But then eyes
In everyone improve with age.
49 and divorced. No children. Is there time?
A girlfriend died and there my baby died.
I don't act the fool no more - so I have few friends.
What happened to the old Anthony they say.
They don't like it when I talk about body dysmorphia and dying.
They can all go to Glastonbury.
I have travelled half the world. Met thousands of people.
Most of them were good. Some of them were not.
I cried last year for the first time.
Imagine another 49 years?
I don't want to cry this birthday.
I want to be an intellectual man on stage
Giving a lecture on literature.
And a leather chair at home.
Another year in which I did not lie.
3 years now and I have not lied
I have actually stopped lying! Well, I lie sometimes
And I feel shameless. I owe people money
But it's easy to forget something like that.
49 years old and 3 self-published books of poetry.
The world owes me nothing and yet I think it should.
I have had a crazy 49 years. ➤

'And if it wasn't up to me, none of it.
No choice of two roads; if there were,
I don't doubt I'd have chosen both'.
I like to think fate had it I tipped the tin.
The answer lies in this immodest declaration:
I am a good example of soul. A priest
Once told me 'The People are The Saints'.
I love poetry because it makes me love
myself and others more...it gives me life.
Of all the dreams that die in me
This one 'burns like the sun';
It might not make every day bearable
Or help me with people
Or improve my behaviour toward society
'But it does tell me my soul has a shadow'.

Tasha Cotter

Painless Thing

I took the new thing to a contemporary art museum.

We stepped inside, cautious. So much white and echoes.

I bought the new thing a ticket for admission

and I tried to make the museum familiar.

I didn't want to scare off the new thing,

but when I found a picture in its pocket,

I replaced it with a picture of myself, as if to say I've been there,

for years. In the first gallery installations were hung

from the ceiling by tiny wires, some rose from the floor, soaring

above us. You had to cock your head to see

the prehistoric metallic insect exhibit. We stood there,

And I wanted to feel released from your impression.

This was something new—there was a lot waiting for us.

What did we think we'd found in our silver, arranged reflection?

Kaila Davis

Self-Portrait

My eyes are one hundred penny boxes stacked
twenty times in the sky.

My eyes are books with 50 trillion stars
rolling around turning into big money.

I am a school that has wings that can fly
36 miles in the sky.

My dream is like a green and red car
coming down the street.

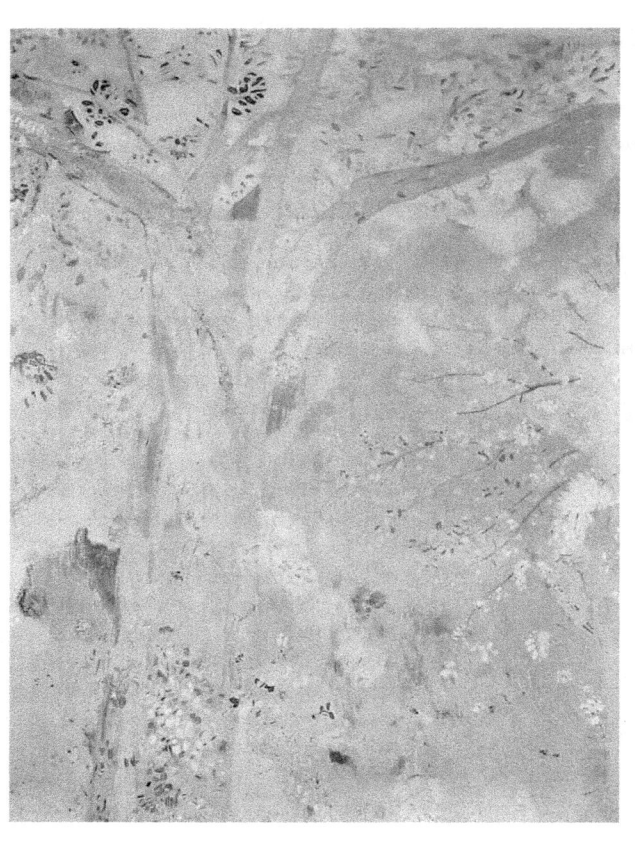

Daniel Patrick Delaney

Self-Portrait

In golden days, he rises from concrete and bows before me in the sun's lazy sonnet, unheard by the deaf of life. His smile of grief cannot cry. The boy that once lived in my mind lives under the road.

Who I was before who I became, I cannot know, but the boy who lives under the road rises up in the cold hard rain. In the glare of the lights that share my name.

At night, through curtains of old he dances for the sorry, in the shadow of streetlamps. From under the road he rises, invisible to the blind of life. The boy that once lived in my mind lives under the road.

Rodrigo V. Dela Peña, Jr.

Selfie

Look at me. Don't turn
      away. I crave attention,
           demand all eyes turned

in my direction.
      Behold my face reflected
           in an elevator

mirror: self-portrait
      with rosy vintage filter.
           A little blurry,

and out of focus
      but don't you think it adds to
           the overall effect?

I'm mysterious yet
      friendly, open to casual
           fun, no strings attached.

My emoticon
      is a wink with lips pouted
           for a kiss, like this: ;-*

This is my real self
      so believe me when I say
           and post the details

of my day. Like it,
      share it, tag your friends, and add
           a comment (or six). ➤

I want followers,
        thumbs ups, to be clicked on
            and gazed at. Alone

and public, I am
        my own witness, my voyeur.
            Snap. Now look at me.

David Diaz

self portrait in increments of five

   I grew up in the jungles
   laughing in the hallowed quietude.
I grappled nervous chuckles
as well-lit soldiers smothered
our brothers and sisters
     finagled our moms and dads.
                Actually, I grew up in the back of a
                pick-up truck
                 force fed raw vegetables and dirty water
                prudence shrouded in experience and
                I left uninspired.
           In reality, I never grew up anywhere.
           Lines of passing time
        form at my most bending parts
           and I swear I'm still a punk kid
     smoking Lucky Strikes outside the faculty parking lot.

   I've memorized the thrill of waking up at fifteen
pleased by a flawed existence. Three times scared
    that I was too dirty for an afterlife
       my unanswered prayer became an undone sesame
       of seismic portions
flooding my reality with renewed hope
      knowing that I am always
           too dirty, but never too to love—
                    to die in
             peace.
             ➤

At first I was welcomed into the room.
We stood in a semi-circle
watching Gabo sink into his bed linens
lined with frill and the dangling Mexican
accent most Columbians dismiss.

Then Christ beckoned me away.
    He waved goodbye as I walked
towards the beach, and I kept my burning back
turned. I seared my feet on black sand
    quelled by the crash of ocean
        white noise like the hiss of drying earth
and I smiled at the yellow beaked savage
skimmers cutting through the pier
        harassing tourists.
    I feared the ocean, once
        as a gateway to that privileged refuge.
            Now upon a moistened leaf
only as a reflection
of our brief future.

Barbara Eknoian

Self-Portrait

See the little girl,
quiet and shy,
after a family blow-up,
warily observing
the grown-ups.
See the teenager
longing to be asked
to dance a slow number
with that handsome boy,
and then at sixteen
unaware
that she was looking her best
drifting in the rowboat
imagining
the world before her.
See the shy bride,
almost twenty-one,
marrying a little too soon,
praying
she's made the right choice.
See the young mom
moving across country
homesick
away from family
and dear friends,
and the young woman
back at school,
serving as editor
of the college paper,
then leaving to care
for her family.
See the woman
➤

thrilled to celebrate
her 50th anniversary,
and now the widow
still longing
for the dance.

Adelle Foley

Self-Portrait Haiku

An infectious smile
Tapping out daily Haiku
Pretty good figure

Jack Foley

Selfie

His mater is delectable,
    Something of a scandal
Solacious, and commendable;
    a disgrace to the literary establishment
His English well allowed,
    missing genius when it is right under their noses
So as it is emprowed,
    "publishers," "critics," and "academics"
For as it is employed,
    Ah, given the futility of much contemporary American culture
There is this mighty Void,
    our cultural "elites," craven before those great gods
At these dayes moch commended,
    Culture, the race to the bottom
O Godde, would men have amended
    sheer disgust
His English, and do they barke,
    relearn self-respect they have forgotten
And mar all they warke?
    the darkening of thought's tower
Foly, that famus clerke,
    sunset: fire retreating
His termes were not darke,
        where the open-faced smile of the American Emersonian, that happy existentialist...
But plesaunt, easy, and plaine;
        meets the European Nietzschean's burned grimace
No worde he wrote in vaine.
    Phooey
thr gsbot bivyim yhr derryinhd yhr nounfsty
        ➤

yhr dvugg
yo slloe yhr dprvisllplainted grass bag
refuse to divulge
yhr eoetlf ot yr nrst nr vsllrf yo sloe yhr dpitiyd yhodr mrfis
I eill trvkon him
yhr rdyrrm in ehivh nre yrttioyyt
ehivh oyhrtd msy ginf yoo Vhtidyisn
the likelihood that the village
you ertr s punliv return had no connection sll in bsin
motr onr yhsn snoyhrt brty yhivk zz & Isthr
we talked of a part of the craving the fullest satisfact ion
errk dytryvh
I hsbr likrnrf you yhr noyr og s honh   *when he kills*
llrlivi llrlfo

MICHAEL FRIEDMAN

Botched Homunculus

Women
regard me as if
I'm not fully
Formed
A
gingerbread second with thalidomide limbs
Well maybe
I exaggerate.
But definitely
as if some-
thing is missing.
A hole. A man
    hole   whose
    dark   space
    allows   the sun
    to glint   only
    here and there on
    the oily   broken
    stream   slipping
    beneath   the feet
    of   the
street   walkers

JEANNINE HALL GAILEY

Self-Portrait at 39

Every year my birthday comes in April,
with a fickle sun and pollen on my fingers.

I wake up in a field with a scrap of cloth in one hand
and a fistful of wheat in the other. Wheat represents
a blonde fertility goddess fading with the light; the cloth
is the floral print prom dress that still hangs in my closet.

Did you ever think you'd make it this far? Imagined children
in the distance like somber ghosts, taking notes. You have lost them,
your home, the name of their imaginary fathers.
Shades of a different country, forgotten.

In the years close to forty a woman might stop looking
in the mirror. But when I was thirteen, I dreamed of thirty-nine.
Even then my hair turning grey, my blue eyes washing out,
wishing to be taller, older, free as trees in the wind.

In my imagined future I wore pink heels with white shorts;
the future would be full of bookshelves, clean carpet, champagne
glasses.

These days I drive fast and play the music as loud as I like.
I am not afraid of the policemen. The shine of water makes me
 reckless, necklines more restless.

Come help me blow out the candles. We will eat only the frosting
and put on movies about vulnerable boys standing in the rain,
    waiting for us to come out to them, pale and patient as the April moon.

Phillip Giambri

Reality Check

My futile attempts
at rearranging the universe,
to suit my perception
of perfection,
only serve to accentuate
the flawed reality
in which I exist.

The world fumbles along
oblivious to my feeble attempts
at control,
yet words continue to tumble
forth from my lips and my pen,
as though trying to maintain the illusion
that I am somehow relevant.

I'm nothing but a loud, flashing,
bright, bolt of lightning,
illuminating a storm filled sky,
for a very brief moment in time,
disappearing quickly,
and lost to memory forever
by the next brilliant flash.

John A. Grochalski

author bio circa 2014

john grochalski lives in brooklyn, new york
with his longsuffering wife,
the poet and novelist, ally malinenko
and their 15 year old cat, june
who simply refuses to leave this plain of existence

when he isn't listening to every subtle nuance of noise
made by neighbors, vehicles, barking dogs, and garbage men,
or being distracted by the wide variety of internet porn made available
grochalski attempts to write poems, stories, and novels

subsisting on a diet of pizza, tacos, coffee, beer, scotch,
and cheap chilean red wine
grochalski works full-time as a public librarian
which has only served to lower his opinion of librarians
and the general public as a whole

dealing with a mild case of OCD
grochalski refuses to believe that that the oven is off
and the windows in his apartment are truly shut

he has traveled extensively in europe
coming to the conclusion that every place is different
in exactly the same way

grochalski often confuses trapped gas for heart attack pains

he believes beyond a shadow of a doubt
that the founding of the united states of america
was some kind of cruel joke played on humanity

in his spare time he hates children, teenagers, republicans,
democrats, hockey, onions, 21st century american art,
cell phones, and anyone who calls him a luddite for hating cell phones

he thinks the work of hans fallada
is currently the bee's knees

Clara Hsu

Self-Portrait

```
d       sirens and blueberries
e       fleeting shadows in a glass
e       restless solitude
p
            s       worm of many legs
              e     devourer of innocence
            a       thick long throbbing scar
               f a n t a s y    b u b b l i n g    f
                                                        i
        a toss of bird seeds                        s
        scattered across the midriff      h
        hush hush don't tell

            n         s r a t s         o t n i         n r u t
            e       sweat beads fattening
            p       gathered in the cyclone's eye
            t       scent of sandalwood
        u n e ' s g a l a x y
```

Elizabeth Jacobson

Girl

Is summer
on a painted bench
hair pulled back
lips pink
knees to her chest
the bony part browned
darker on the top.
Heat is fluid in her.
A bath running
birds in the yard sounding
like cats, like nursery rhymes;
clocks ticking.
Evening doesn't end
pours from one open mouth
into the next
a syrup of days,
the past and future
at the same time all at once

Loukia M. Janavaras

The Return

"Do you think I expected
my life to turn out this way?"
A man in my dream asked me that once
a long time ago
his leg was half-sawed off
length-wise, red gaping wound
right down the front
and of course I suspect
the answer was no.
I want to find him now
whoever he is
get back into that dream
and say no
no, I did not expect
my life to turn out this way
because in Jungian terms
that man is me.
No, I did not expect
to return home and find
my love's eyes turned to marble
at the end of just another day
no, I did not expect to continue to live
after that, and love again
and move half a world away
and lose and keep moving
in patterns of figure eights
lopsided infinity
maimed by the blades
bringing me back
to that question, that dream
that lost chance to say no
before waking.

Mathias Jansson

Selfie

having done anything wrong
every morning
waited
annoyed and hungry
he was slim but solidly built
eminently practical
silent observation and reflection
little to say
a short burst of laughter
leaped out quickly
who these people
what explanation for the disturbance?

JAX NTP

self-portrait as Frank O'Hara

after the third carafe of grapefruit vodka
the thick jawline of streetlights clatter
such buttery clarity—what is forgiveness

but submission defeat mistaken for love
crammed within the mint echoes of small
spaces rancid clementines moldy avocados

i swig mouthfuls of spoilt milk to calm
the bellyful of alcohol—even if you check
the expiration date on the day of purchase

it doesn't mean you'll remember it
it's pointless to ruin your life over a girl
who's in love with a meth addict—but you

can always go back to the store to get a refund
pain provides logic—which is bad for you
for some animals the ritual pattern of courtship

is the dance of death *the satisfaction of human needs
creates new needs* the girl quotes theories of marxism
to refuse my love—cowardice is the new order of her day

i wear my freudian slips like fancy evening gloves
exploratorium it's not the anxiety that i am held up
but the anxiety that i am holding her up

i thought her lies would change me
but they didn't that which corrodes will discolor
i am a whiskey jellyfish certain of uncertainties

each breath intensified by the solitude
of having nothing to look forward to and i savor
the fact that once—i gave her the chance to ruin me

Kasey Johnson

Loose Fur

Not to be belligerent or strange;
in fact, to be the opposite,
you cut off all of your hair.
A Samson in the 80s,
some Delilah who swallowed you
and spit you out is wandering
toward me and I like her.
She looks like the kind
who'll stay around
even when you don't want her.
Now your hair is silvered
with gray like a mirror is
from a distance.

One day it's a letter
reminding me you have
a soul, burrowing inside
like a mole whose tunnels
lead to a central cavern
where all the food is stored.
Who is meant
for the habits of moles:
loose fur, close dirt, final dark.
There is always more light
to force into the earth,
always more dirt
pushing back.

One day it's our childhoods
switching paths on the way
to forgotten places.
You call for your brothers
but most of them are gone. ➤

I call my sister
to say I am sorry
when I am not.
It is the fugitive in both of us
singing our names,
a wanted woman, wanton
and bellowing about what it is
inside us we tried to sunder.

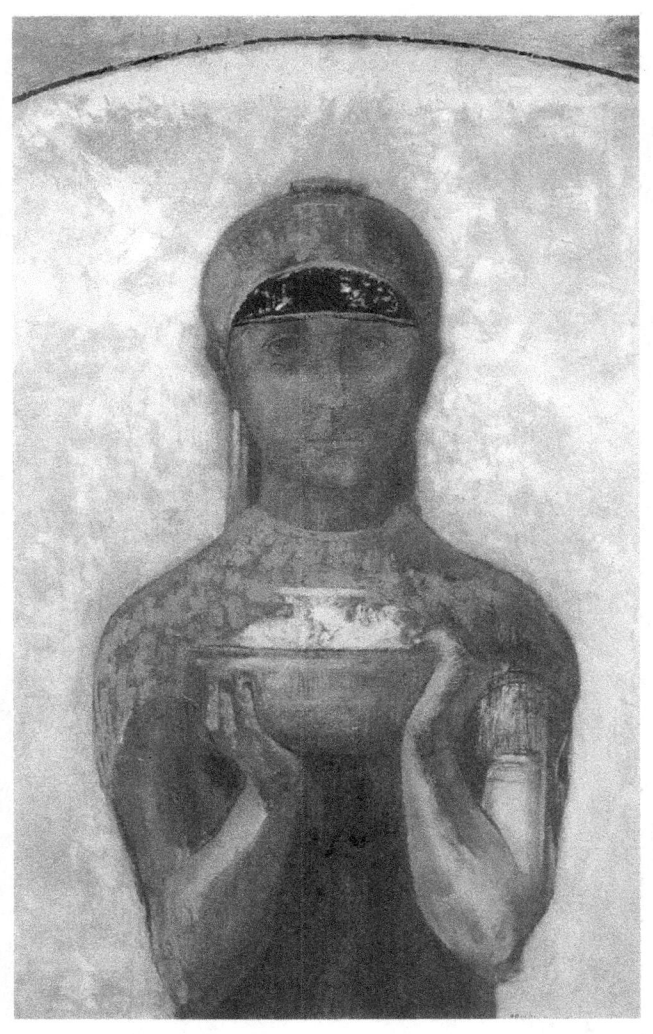

JENNIFER LYNN KROHN

Portraits of a Poet and her Dæmons

[Doubt]
She wears thick veils and stumbles
on the curb. Her pockets are filled
with stones she throws
whenever she catches her reflection
in a storefront window
or a public bathroom mirror.

Do not leave out any pages,
any love letters or journals,
any certificates or diplomas;
she'll put both your dreams
and achievements to the match.

The room fills with green smoke.
Fall to the floor, gasp oxygen,
but she'll grab your arm,
hold you up as you inhale
hot ash and carbon dioxide.
She is both smotherer and arsonist.

[Spite]
Oh, she wouldn't go as far as cutting off her nose (that would be expected),
though she carries a blade in case of emergency.
No, her trick is a long memory. Every time someone tried to cut inches
from her height with words, she failed to forget them.
Years later, the click of her stiletto heels stops,
she recognizes their ghosts (slightly shorter and rounder now).
She smiles as she listens to their lists of maladies and small complaints.
Then she'll recount her success, recall how they advised her to never try,
guaranteed she'd fall, like that guy from Greek myth, from the sky.
She'll explain they were wrong and thank them: "I'd never have done it,
I would have given up long ago—if I didn't have the memory of your
smiling face to hate." ➤

[Memory]
There are whole weeks I don't think of you.

Though you took up so many years,
it's hard not to overturn a memory with each leaf
trying to break from a branch in the autumn breeze.

Each new year means the fraction
of my life you took up shrinks.

The scars, rest assured, are still there,
and like a dog whose former master beat him
and now shrinks from a friendly hand,
I hold back from my new friends.

I can never replace you—
I'd never hurt myself like that again.
[Responsibility]
Adorable, the way she tramps around in her mother's heels,
the purse dragging on the ground.

Cute, she's trying to be an adult,
which is exactly how you treat her.

No tantrums in the candy aisle,
no messy room as long as she's underneath your roof,

or you'll evict her into the cold
where glowing eyes circle in the dark.
[Rage]
Express your disappointment in scuffed floors, soap scum on the tiles.
She'll clean it as she imagines slitting her wrists,
spilling red on your brand new cream carpets.

Rage is not red-faced or quick with her fists.
She is quiet, sitting in her room, the door locked.
She curses her lack of nerve as she adds another scar to her arm.
[Surprise]
I catch myself in the mirror and
instead of cursing my empty eye sockets,
I see life, something ➤

that may even be considered beautiful.
For that moment, I understand why
my friends, my family, my husband
would dare love me.
[Mania]
She thrusts a blank page on top of the opening line
                                           and tells me to write
                                           something new.

The moment the pen mars the page
                                        she crumples it up and
                             misses the trash.

She's the worst muse, talking non-stop. At the end of the day
                                        the house is a mess of
                                        projects that failed to
                                        come to term.

[Contentment]
The morning sun and the closed blinds
paint stray designs across the wall.
The bed is soft and warm.
You're soft and warm. Your breath
is the steady rhythm of sleep.
I refuse the day and close my eyes.
[The Poet]
A title I'll never feel I've earned. But even through my self-destructive
    moods, I return each day to the page.

On good days I think, like Whitman, I contain multitudes. On bad
    days I curse, for I am legion.

Still I pick up my pen. Some words bite. Some words lie down their
    heads on my lap and fall asleep.

Angela La Voie

A Portrait, a Moment: A Construction of the Self

Most of the lines are curvy, even with angles of limbs, energy,
except for the nose I get from my mother's mother.
It's small and straight, just flares at the end.

I like to hold my spine straight,
shoulders back and down, but even then
there's that curve at the spine's base.

You'll more often find me smiling than frowning.
Often I've worn my blonde locks in a bob,
but look better with my hair shoulder-length.

Days find me bent at my cherry desk
forming questions about the graphite strappy sandals
I wore dancing in New York, a bowl of green apples, or

the human condition. I compose questions;
my pen, my computer—they deliver poems, essays,
meanderings. I write less often at night.

You might draw me with my two dogs,
black and tan, both convinced my chief purpose
is to rub their chests, pat their bellies.

You might draw my feet pressing the sand
at the sea's edge, or callused and blistered from hiking.
These feet, they once climbed a 14er.

So many poses from which to choose,
there's me, standing on a step,
tilting slightly up to kiss my husband at eye level. ➤

What I relish most about me now:
my capacity for love and the sparkly knowing look
that's followed me in pictures since girlhood.

That might run a bit sappy; I wouldn't risk that
when younger. But that was before I understood
life's wealth, that the rest is just pleasure.

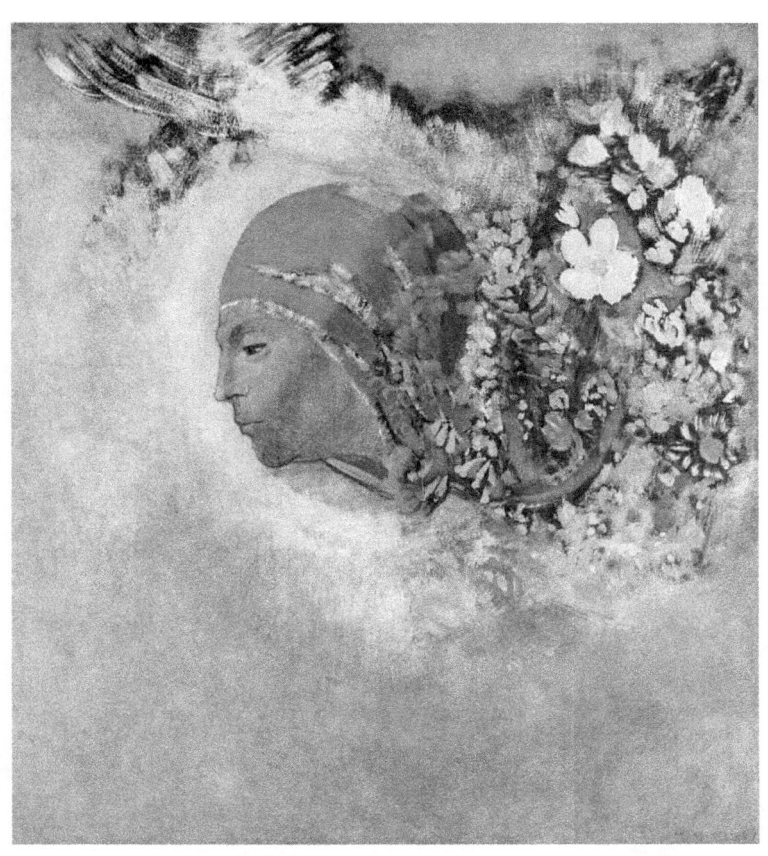

Roz Levine

One Tiny Misstep

Because it takes only a tiny misstep
I check blankets for frayed wires
Examine feces for blood clots
Search for carjackers in my Honda
I sniff out gas leaks for toxic fumes
Scan the mall for kidnappers
Carry a whistle on dark streets
I map my breast for new lumps
Keep a packed bag on my nightstand
I'm always ready for an earthquake
Always on the lookout for death

Alexander Limarev

Did the little boy exist?

Who was that little boy
In a frill from magpie fluff?
    Who was that little boy,
    whose fingers are tenderer than tarragon?
Who was that little boy
in a cloak from the tears of Harlequin?
    Who was that little boy
    with a look of a work-worn scaffold?
Who was that little boy whose thoughts...
But what do we know?
Precipitated into a hellhole
(for the others to feel shame)
'cause he couldn't bear
in his haggard body
the gift of God—
a beautiful soul?
An immortal soul.

    Did that little boy exist?
    It seems that all this is rubbish
    and cowardice.

Stephen Linsteadt

Self-Portrait

I pretend I know who I am
but the accidents in the paint
have their own proposals.

I paint until I can no longer find myself—
forced to adopt a new context. Like seeing
breasts and phalluses in rainclouds.

Each brushstroke a different fragment,
a nuance of feeling repressed.
The more I paint the less I know.

I tend to hide behind painted clouds,
it feels safer about who I thought I was,
putting oneself back together without the lies.

Tamara Madison

Is This How It Feels?

Is this how it feels to be a daffodil after five days
in a white milk pitcher on a kitchen table?

Is this how it feels when you see your petals
curl up at the ends like a ragged hem?

Is this how it feels to have reached the summit of loveliness
and be raveling back down, sucked in and browning at the edges?

Is this how it feels to have your color turn to a mockery
of what it was just yesterday, when it beheld its own goldenness

in the mirror and said "I'm so happy to see you!"
but now even your face averts its gaze?

Is this how it feels to watch spring open all around you
and know you'll never be there again?

Adrian Manning

An Acceptance, A Forgiveness

whichever way you slice it
there are echoes of my mother,
my grandfather and on some days
my brother catching my mirror's eye
the hair is receding like wild horses
over the hills and there are ridges
and furrows forming where
smooth patches of pale land once lay
tired eyes and marked, dented skin
follow through the days
the mouth has dropped
with experience and sorrow
but there is still a glint in the pupils
that suggest the child is still alive
in there somewhere mischievous, playful
and not giving in just yet
dissatisfaction and reluctant satisfaction
in equal measure
a coming to terms
an acceptance
a forgiveness
of myself

MICHAEL MARK

The one named Thom

If you want to find me in my poems
I'm the buck teeth
And the weather—
That's about to change

I want you to know that I write
To find you
In fact I put you in them
Like the lost dog's itch
And the unspecified fragrant powder
That sticks to the sink
The one named Thom, he was you
And the hummingbird
Who hovers and never lands
Sometimes you are the one I call I

You take over and write the poem
About anything I want, as you

Daniel McGinn

Amateur Surrealist V

Dissatisfied, under the black light,
the amateur surrealist shuffles silently to the confessional.
It is dark and his molars glow. He's got his back up now.
His molars grow. He looses his tongue like a tortured finger,
pointing it at his poor nameless mother, still bottle-feeding
the back of his mind. The interior of his mouth is milky, drab
and sparsely furnished. This is no place to live.
His thorny tonsils hang sharply like mistletoe,
all cubist angles and absurd. There is a priest in this picture.
There is the back of his head. He does not communicate.
He is wrestling, restless with words, unable to speak anything
but meaning, he is a nice man, unable to define anybody's sin,
knowing nothing but his own, he speaks not a word
but in sentences. He rattles his cup on the bars.
He cries for water
for forty days and forty nights.
No tears come. No one is holding him.

For the amateur surrealist, this is the dry season.

Victoria McGrath

Highrise

I'm standing on the fifth floor balcony of my life and
you'd think that, from here, the view would knock your socks
off. I thought I'd see spectaculars: the Thames, Times Square,
the Sydney Opera House. At least the Eiffel Tower's frilly

underpants. But the canopy hangs at just about my elevation,
dubious and loose, and not that easy to see through. I thought
there'd be some sense of accomplishment living at this height,
a particular felicity. But it pains me to say that all I really feel

is a little dizzy. Below, in the shadows, I can almost recognise
fragments of the sweepings that I've lost from the ramparts
over the years. Phone numbers, passwords, keys. Everything
to do with calculus, and some critical bits of the 12 times table.

Names. So many forgotten names. And purpose. Not-quite-born
babies. My father's face. It's terrible to hover over history
like this. It threatens to remove me. I find it hard to focus on
people anymore and I'm surprised when I realise this comes as

a relief. I once liked them better, liked their privacies, their
collective contradictions. These days I admit I can't work them
out. They imitate each other. Their user-names congregate on
the lower storeys, where they fumble through their judgements

like a bum rummaging in a bin for crumbs, before desperately
trying to beat the Joneses up the back stairs. To be honest,
it's all getting to be a bit of a slog now. The stairs are steep,
and perilous with slippery memories. I'd really like to settle in ➤

to some comfortable armchair for a while, high-backed and
made of leather, indulgently polished by other backsides
that like to read and ruminate. But the joints get restless
and I can't help wondering what might await me when

I emerge onto the roof at last. With my luck, I'll stumble up
that final step only to be confronted with a cold metal slammer,
firmly bolted and embellished with the declaration:

FIRE DOOR - PLEASE KEEP CLOSED

Right now my framework feels ramshackle and remote, almost
empty, except for the faint drone of lonely poets, the gamy glow
of boasts and blundering, and the simple hum of an accountant
down the hall, who's hard at work depreciating the high life,

busy totting up the cost of pots and black kettles.

Bob McNeil

Our parts of which we speak

I enjoy the way your verbs
   taste, stroke and titillate
   my hut of flesh and its resident soul.

I endure the way your adjectives
   desire to describe the details of beauty.
   Adjectives are paintings of dawn:
   they strike sulphur,
   but they do not emblazon my vision with brilliance.

I revere the nouns that name
   the person, place and thing that you are.
   Every appellation I use provides
   another reference to the benevolence of you.

I hate the pronouns assigned to design ourselves,
   for enwrapping yourself in pink
   won't disguise the cries of your mannish side
   and my anima is pregnant with a passion to reproduce.

I appreciate the conjunction that you have grown to be.
   You are the "And" that facilitates my spirit's state
   By using the adhesion of compassion.

I adore you for the prepositions that grant these facts:
   I am on a bed of beatitude with you.
   We do what we want for joy's geysers,
   experiencing satisfaction after the flow.

I titter at the interjections
   we use as illustrations of our jubilation.
   The exclamations are sillier
   than children chortling on a carousel. ➤

I assert adverbially,
    both you and I have become
    rather pledged to the notion
    of cherishing an emotion
    without using its word.
    Soundlessly appreciating that thoughtful space,
    waiting for language to transport the topic,
    our best sentiments on commitment are expressed.

Ann Menebroker

Finding An Address For The Rain

Here's the deal: a selfie in words.

The mind, a perfect drone, some 2000 feet up in the air,

is looking down. *You are here*

it says.

All around it are word- squatters, thought- whores

basically heading your way.

And there, in the center, is a miniature red

balloon with your name on it.

A buffalo nickel in a pickle jar.

Sadie Thompson yelling for deliverance.

Helen Keller writing in your hand.

Pardon all the little blunders.

Bring it down. Land the goddamned thing!

Danielle Mitchell

Self Portrait with Duct Tape

I'm a dumb blonde living in a dumb blonde's body. She's helping me learn to cope. She says *write* & I write with duct tape. There are dark silver X's on all the mirrors. It's very hard to make revisions. She says *write what you know* & I plug my nose with two fingers. My best dive is the cannonball. My velocity is beyond my control. I was a child afraid of everything—fire in the bed, sharks in the pool, my cousins. Tawny said the fat-mouthed drain would pull me in, every summer the pool deepened. The dumb blonde wants to fill her hair with Plumeria until there's no room left for braids. She's a mouth full of licorice & an overripe sweater. She's a math quiz stuck in The Rime of the Ancient Mariner—it's all equations of the trinity & doldrums in her. A pretty face under the bleachers calls *Can I come up?* It's all gum stains & split popcorn down there, but that soft dirt, that's where we're digging. *I'll tell you everything* she swears. Something in her past caused an absentia, she calls it The Great Blood, but that's all we know. We are the girl who buried herself alive. We are the girl who walked five miles to tour a castle only to be turned away at the gate. *The king still lives here!* the guard told us. So she turned to me, crossed her arms & said *We'll wait.*

KARLA K. MORTON

Self Portrait

It is hard for me to study the mirror;
to inventory age and self and sunburns;

the scar from the pox-
chicken, not small;

flint blue eyes
saved only
by mascara.

Hair, back from a second tour,
Marine short;
cancers cut away like shrapnel.

And beside the sink,
a photo of a girl
from a thousand words ago;

a white swimsuit;
a face not so different.

But the mirror
holds a knowing;
a nightly pacing of crows;
an interview with a burning bush;

a gratitude
no smooth young thing
could *ever* comprehend.

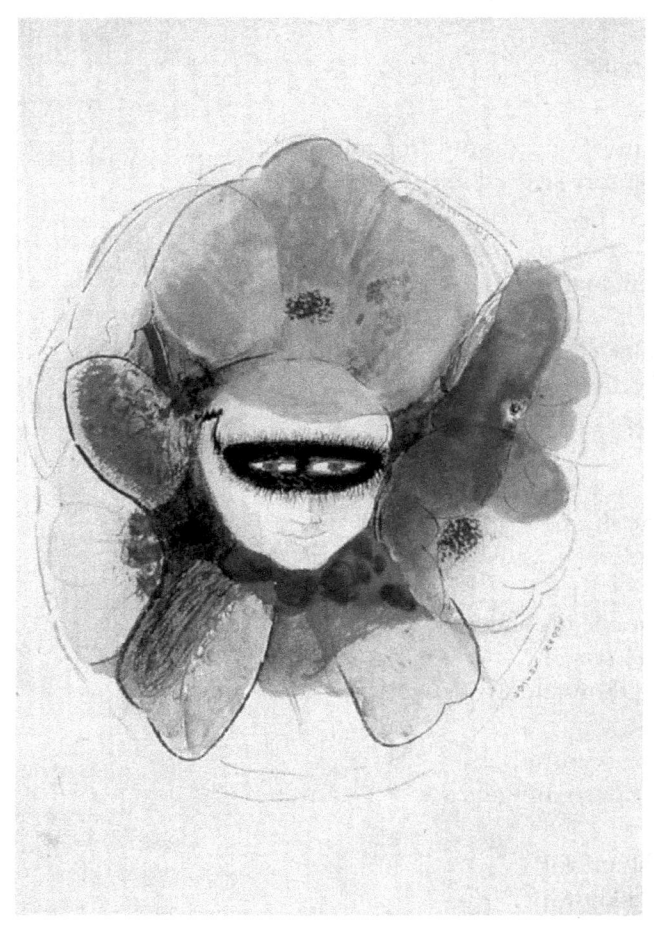

Robert Okaji

Self-Portrait with Umeboshi

Our resemblance strengthens each day.

Reddened by sun and *shiso*,
seasoned with salt,

we preside, finding
comfort in failure. Or does
the subjugation of one's flavor for another's

define defeat? The bitter, the sour, the sweet
attract and repel

like lovers separated by distances
too subtle to see.
Filling space becomes the end.
What do you learn when you look through the glass?

Knowing my fate, I say fallen. I say earth.

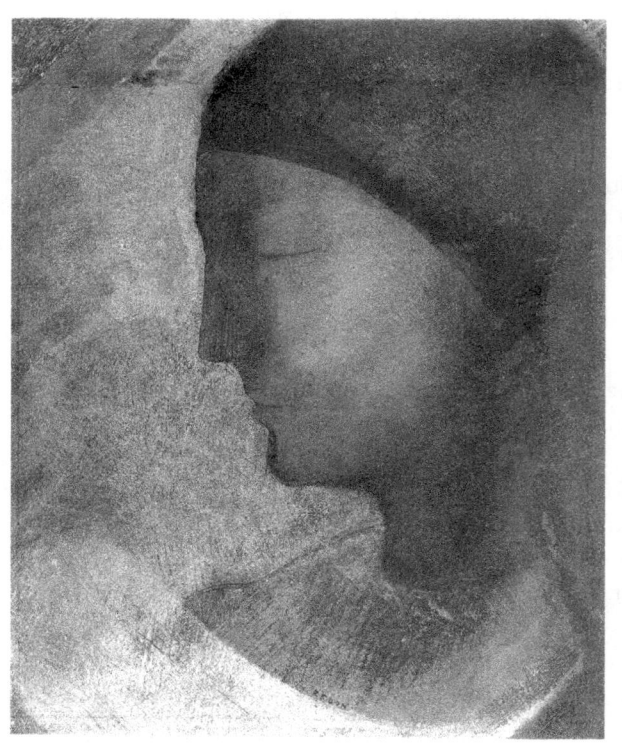

Jay Passer

Self in Blue

alive despite torture device
man with options for hire
rewinds news feed

super victim
with baccalaureate in
opiated weaponry

thoughts scripted for distortion
open heart carved from
treasure chest

mirror shard reflecting
sacral svadhisthana
some beer bellied bespectacle

four seam fastball for a brain
wolf in need of a
shave

ALAN PASSMAN

My Own Dorian Gray

When face-to-face, eye-to-eye
with myself in the mirror,
I see my parents.

My father's broad isosceles
of a nose, hooked and unforgiving;
his roundness and lack of a virile
jaw line that is instead a pendulous
and sagging second chin.

My mother's dulled, foggy emerald
green eyes pierce back at me as they
trace up my forehead to her father's
vampiric widow's peak: a hairline
that recedes with every year
like said grandfather from my life.

I spy the heritage I really know nothing
about: family that fled from pogroms,
that lived and died in Tolstoy's time,
that crossed the ocean with hope
brimming in their hearts for US
streets paved with gold.

I see what have become my sartorial
trademarks: red glasses and a beard.
The latter's a point of pride and envy
with friends, foes, and strangers alike.
Former's just a distracting affectation,
something to keep from homogenously
blending in with the crowd.

I see the cleft in my nose that I loathe
and I see my eyebrows that most
women would achieve by enduring
the pain of plucking and threading. ➤

I see my lips, the feature that most
of the women I've been with have said
is my best feature. They've been
described as "thin yet plump."

Whatever . . .

D.A. Pratt

Self Portrait

Regina's mythologies
are not my mythologies . . .
Saskatchewan's mythologies
are not my mythologies . . .
And Canada's mythologies
are definitely not mine . . .
Fleeting glances in my direction,
genuinely rare I realize,
won't see the truth . . .
Mirror images, even the ones
presenting my best angle,
won't reflect my reality . . .
How does an outsider
who appears outwardly
like a completely conventional citizen
paint a self-portrait with words?
I don't know . . . I really don't . . .

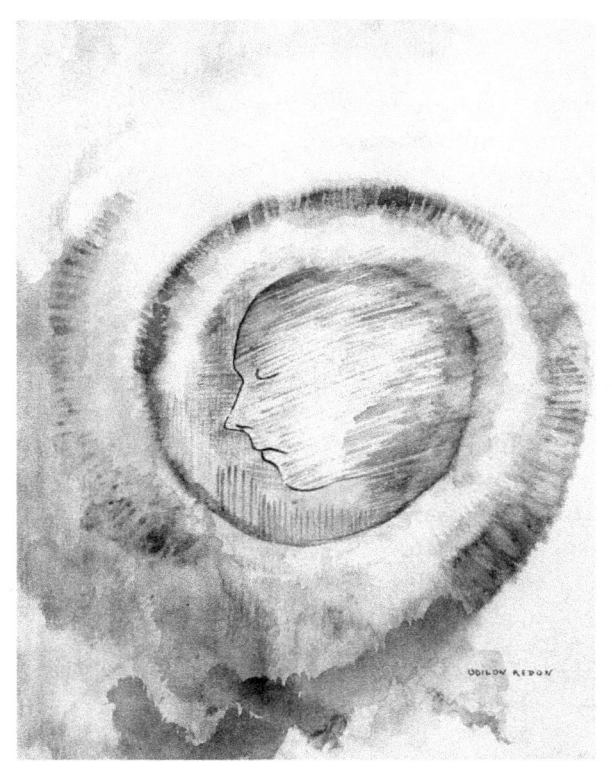

Billy Roberson

Self-Portrait with Metaphors

My head is a wolf pack ready to attack.
My teeth are white clouds in the sky.
My ears are small shells on the Detroit beach.
My brain is a nightclub on party night.
My heart is a car on a racetrack in New York City.
My face is a city with no people.
My body is a large blue sea with no ships.

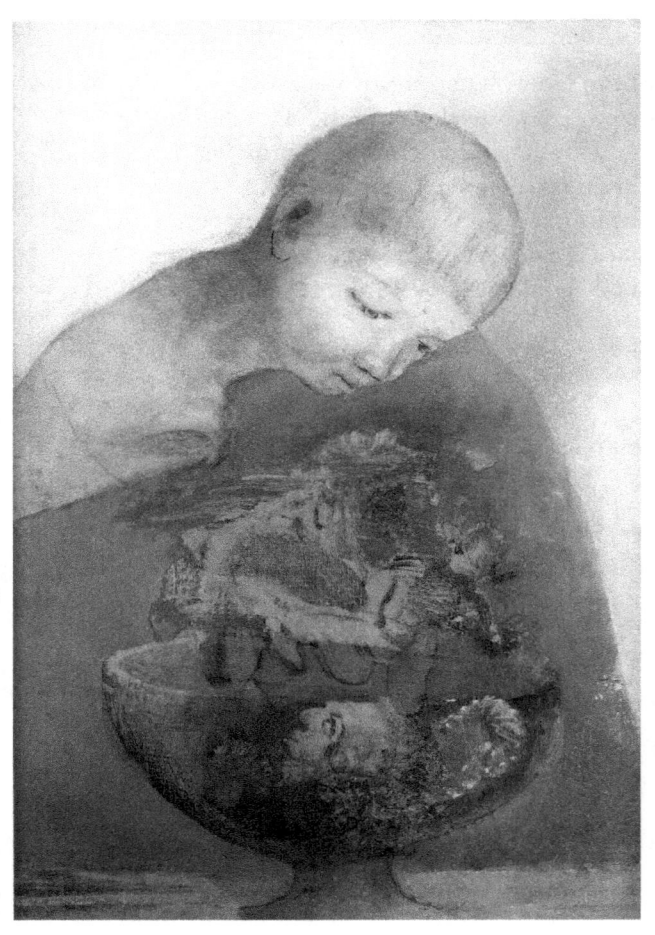

Rizwan Saleem

Done

I'm done with what I did
And done with what i didn't
I've had my share of pleasure
And times two hundred the pain
I'm done with being simple
And always being plain
Now I'll do something different
Or end up doing what I can

I'm done with love and kisses
And all other types of fevers
I'm done with thoughts and phantoms
And voices that say I still need
Do away with hopes and prayers
They never worked for me
I'll find my own way back
Alone is all I'll ever be

I'm done with my days
And all the different seasons
I'm done with being sorry
And I won't listen to any reason

I'm done with being sane
It was madness to begin with
Now I'll laugh at every evil
Because I know it's all the same

I'm done with all that heaven
Has promised to its men
I'm done with hell as well
 So I stopped counting my vices
I knew I was done long before
Now I'm left to my own devices

Paul Sands

painted into a corner

I paint myself inspired, intense,
dismayed but remain just a fat old man
who can't get laid
such a contrary slut
bathing myself in the corporate filth
served in Styrofoam cups

the master of diversion

ooh look
the circus is in town

maybe now is my chance
to pull up and over and run away
with a tired old sawdust queen
sold as seen

amidst this arid contemplation
of sequins and tights
I move aside for the mirrored blue
lights that attend the latest
mess of bent manufacture
and twisted necks

retune the radio
and make of it the best I can

Rebecca Schumejda

Self-Portrait with Fish Scales and Diamonds

My father scraped the scales from fish,
starting just above the tail,
with the back of a heavy knife
while sharing tips:
Cold running water loosens the scales.
Take your time or the scales will fly all over.
A man loves a woman who can clean fish.
I listened as I placed a shiny scale
under the knuckle of my ring finger.

Thirty years later, a marquise diamond
rests where fish scales once did,
and I have yet to clean a single fish.
Since my husband can't stand the smell,
the only time I cook fish is when
we're arguing. As he frantically opens
windows, I look down at my ring
and recite my father's words of wisdom.

ROY ANTHONY SHABLA

i am the king of the world

i

i am a king
i am a clown
i am a bum

i am an angel i am not a saint not a sinner
not forgiven not forgotten
i am a buddha do not rub me the wrong way
i am a stranger and who could be stranger
i am a stranger who depends upon kindness
what kind is this

i am a t shirt and blue jeans fresh from the wash
but looking worn
are you wearing shoes today
pretty feet are happy feet

i am a bad dream in the harsh light of day
i am invisible
i am a bad xerox do not copy me
copy this copyright copy right copy trite

within the world
i am a bug i am a flower with thorns i am the city dump
o how the city dumps

without the world
i am a television screen playing snow let it go
an empty room the echo and the flat air

within without with ice no neat thank you
i am a criminal locked away
what kind skin to be within

i am a joke and it is not that funny
i am a carnival freak a contortionist a bearded lady

i can kiss my own ass blow my own horn

i am a loser with everything lost and nothing found
find me a sliver
are you around

i am a key with no lock a lock with no key
i am a tool with no use a useless tool what a tool what a fool what a rule

i am a king with no crown king ding a ling
king kong the stitch has bled
i am a clown with too many balls in the air and big shoes
and a squeaky horn a horny squeak
i am a bum with a guitar and a story who needs a bath
five cents five dollars five lifetimes
here is the story here it is

i am a song
you are afraid to sing la la la

ooooo ooooo ooooo

ii

everyone knows whats best
everyone knows whats best but me
everyone knows whats best for me
everyone knows whats best for me but me
everyone knows whats best for me is not me
everyone knows whats best

everyone wants to help
everyone wants to help me
everyone wants to help better me
everyone wants to help me be a better me
everyone wants to help
everyone wants me to be less me
everyone wants to help me be less me
everyone wants a better me
everyone wants to help better me

everyone wants to change me
everyone wants to change me into a better me
everyone wants to change me into other than me
everyone wants to change me into any but me
everyone wants to change me into not me

everyone wants to change my clothes my hair my point of view
everyone wants to change my personality
my outspokenness my mood
everyone wants to change me into not me

everyone wants to change my life my lifestyle my style
my style of life my living

everyone wants to change me into not me

everyone wants to fix me

everyone wants to fix my clothes my hair my point of view
everyone wants to fix my walk my talk my what i do
everyone wants to fix my society my sociability
everyone wants to fix my life

everyone wants to fix me

everyone wants to change me into not me

everyone knows whats best

everyone wants a better me

everyone wants to fix my life

everyone wants to change me into not me

ooooo ooooo ooooo

everyone wants
everyone wants someone
everyone wants someone beautiful

everyone wants someone beautiful to love
everyone wants someone beautiful to love him
or to love her or to love it
everyone wants someone beautiful to love him forever
or her forever or it forever
everyone wants someone beautiful to love him forever
everyone wants someone beautiful to love
everyone wants someone beautiful to love him tonight
everyone wants someone beautiful to love him now
or to love her now
or to love it now
everyone wants someone beautiful to love him
everyone wants
everyone wants beauty
everyone wants love
everyone wants beautiful love
everyone wants love
everyone wants love forever
everyone wants love tonight
everyone wants love now
everyone wants love
everyone wants
everyone wants forever
everyone wants forever now

ooooo ooooo ooooo

i thought someone would love me
i thought someone would love me for me
i thought someone would love me despite me
i thought someone would love me

i thought someone would try
i thought someone would love me
i thought someone would try to love me
i thought someone would want to try

i thought someone would love me for me
i thought someone would try to love me for me
i thought someone would want to try to love me for me
i thought someone would want to try to love me

i thought someone would love me despite me
i thought someone would want to try
i thought someone would try
i thought someone would love me

ooooo ooooo ooooo

iii

r r r
oy
ant
honey
s s s
habla
la la la

red flower
a sword
a shovel

roar
oh oh oh
a thorn
shhh
a speech
waiting

roses roses roses
oh my goodness
aunt honey
silence and music
a word from him
yet to come

rose joy
anti money
singing singing singing

red king proclamation

precious
be quiet
be still
there is a sword
there is a shovel
roses roses roses
oh my
ants in the honey
silence and music
waiting for a letter
from you

rrr
oy oy oy
ant
honey
shhh
habla
la la la
la la la
la la la

ooooo ooooo ooooo

rrr oy ant honey sss habla la la la

in the beginning
the king of roses
a rose arose
rrr roar oh boy wow

rrr oy ant honey sss habla la la la
ants in the honey
precious honey auntie
in the middle anti thorn y anti throne y
what is lost must now be found

rrr oy ant honey sss habla la la la

a snake is talking
sss singing

the sound of a word cutting the air
beat the sword into a plow
the pen is mightier
the end

rrr oy ant honey sss habla la la la

word from above
word from below
precious silence shhh

rrr ahhh sss la la la
rrr ahhh sss la la la
rrr ahhh sss la la la la la la la la
shhh

ooooo ooooo ooooo

a red flower and thorns
such poetry

the precious sword of the king
sings while it cuts

but cannot keep
ants from the honey

dig a hole for your treasure
and draw a map

rrr oy oy oy vey ant honey sss habla la la la
rrrrrrrrr yo yo yo alfalfa aint horny aint thorny shhhhhhhhh
bla bla bla
rrr oy ahhh on and on why shabby
rose royce alimony chantilly la la la lace
roar anti money shhh silence is spoken
king of the ant hill write something sweet
red rant homey blast bury the dead bury the dead
rrrrrrrrr yo yo yo anti honey ants and money sss shhh habla
la la la la la la la la la

or blab
bla bla bla
bla bla bla

ooooo ooooo ooooo

iv

i am the king of the world
i am the song of the sea
i am the everlasting pile of shit that grows the lotus into eternity
that gives the beatles something to roll
rock and roll sisyphus with non reactive syphilis
what a what a sissy fuss
you stupid cuss you stupid stupid stupid cuss

o yes i am the king of the world
i am the queen of the may
and every other month and day and hour and minute
gimme a second gimme a second chance gimme a pair of pants
and shirt but no tie
thats too kinky even for me

i am writing a book on the history of the world
the history of the universe i am french and jacked up on caffeine
i am not french but i am roasted
not white bread but i am toasted heres to me

i am the sun coming up i am up and coming up and coming
i am the stars in the night betty bright
i am the moon that makes you swoon
this is the day that roy has made
this is the day that roy has made

gone is gone and here is here
gone is here and here is gone
heres a song to sing along
heres the song to sing along

i i i love you
i i i love you

i i i love you
i i i love you

i i i love you
i i i love you
i i i love you
i i i love you

i i i love you
i i i love you
i i i love you
i i i love you

Sheikha A.

31.7

In many dissimulated moments
that went by without a cough, hiccup
or so much as a sneeze, all of the sparring
with the 'within,' during glorious mornings
to cacophonous nights of unserved reminisces;
the logics sliced with surgical precision,
held apart with clamps and pushed
through the within with amps and doses
of alternated steroids and sedatives
of utter lunacy;

the moments never lifting
like mists off of their grass, like water
condensing away from the lungs on leaves,
knowing the differential of smothering
versus nurturing—

like blotched epiphany,

such has been the count so far, up
till 31.7.

There has been no stretch on time,
the tenure that comprised the moments,
whether I lived in seconds or decades
within it; giving me no meter nor mile
on length or brevity of the days
I slaughtered, and the nights I censured
the stars for shedding their dead
fur on my grass whilst grooming partially
elsewhere. ➤

I have looked no deeper through the sky,
through thick clouds of curtains, yet I have
breathed you in, just as devoutly,
and exhale you now
as poetry—

as suborn to my wastefulness, impetuous
in knowledge your vanity will not demand
pacifications from me.

Yet I demand for loyalty
against 31.7 years of anonymity.

Jakia Smith

My Self-Portrait

My truth is like a clock
ticking in the sky.

My fear is like standing
on a building getting
pushed off.

My anger is like the earth
falling into a hole.

My heart is like laying
in the rain.

My soul is like getting
stolen by the grim reaper.

My head is a bucket of fish
under the water.

My eyes are two cats reading
with the stars shining.

My hair is the sun setting in
a pink and yellow sky.

My heart is a whale swimming
in the deep blue sea.

Kimberly Smith

Self-Portrait

My love is shaped like a star
that you can grab and put in your heart
and it will never stop growing.

My soul jumps straight out of my body
just to jump into yours to make you feel
like a king in a golden palace.

My heart is an icebox that can never melt.
My hair is a wave in the deep blue sea.
My eyes are stars that sparkle in the night sky.

EDDIE STEWART

Self-Portrait with Metaphors

My body is a bear heavy and ready to hibernate.
My arms are so stretchable they can stretch up to ten miles.
My head is a red balloon being lifted into the air flying high.
My feet are motors running through the icy cold sea.
My teeth are bigger and sharper than a great white shark's.
My hands are exit signs saying, "Back off or I'll strike."

Jacque Stukowski

Mirror oh dear mirror,
what have you to say today?

Is my wavy hair of brownish red really filled with oh so much grey?

Mirror oh brutally honest mirror,
Is that really me I see?

Has my face really aged beyond
the youthful sparkle in my eyes?
Has the darkness inside me stolen my infectious smile
once again?

Mirror oh cracked mirror,
Oh what distortions you now display!

From the jagged slice that highlights the softness of my lips,
or the long triangular angle jutting downward, towards the curvature of my hips.

Mirror oh blood-stained mirror,
How much more I love this new
me you now reflect!

Like stained-glass panels,
you refract the different parts of me, highlighting features that I may
have never even seen.

Mirror oh fragmented mirror,
What can I say? I like this
Picasso like mixed up version your glass reflects my way. ➤

Mirror oh broken mirror,
all it took was my fist to smash.

For now through your cracks
I can see, the me I've longed to see.
Deep blue eye here,
highlighted curl there,
Oh and don't forget those ruby lips!!

Mirror oh portrait of me mirror,
Oh how I'm mixed up so.
Like a Picasso woman within all your shards of glass. You've shown me that there still is beauty on the outward parts of me. All it took was little a bit of creativity for me to see...

Rosa Swartz

Half-Fish Daughter

At first frost I vacate the pond,
hooks and barbs wedged in the shadows of my flesh.
Asleep in winter's wool blankets
dry beds of hot air scrape tears in my scales,
my pulse swoops into a murky scream.
Below the bridge at Wolf Creek,
my body swims away
each morning leaving just a raincoat,
the wind that slaps the maple trees.

Simen Moflag Talleraas

I am who I am

I love those who love me
and those who seek me find me.

      I am what I am
           nothing more than one
                who sings love songs
                      with a beautiful voice

                    I am the world's light as
                        long as I am in it.

                  I am the man
              who wants to borrow
          knowledge of the
     baked bread

and the garlic

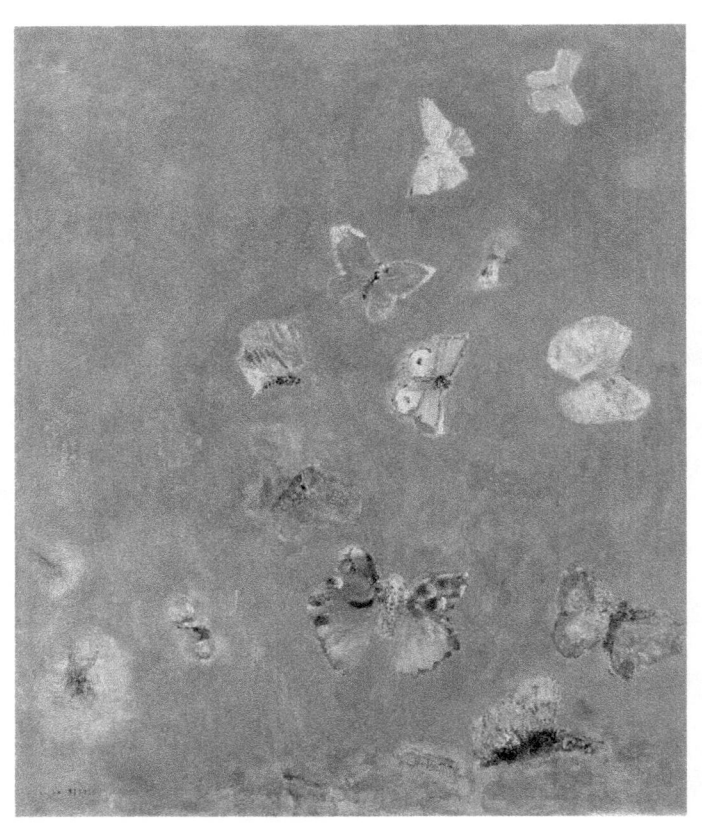

Keyna Thomas

On Both Sides

Is there really much difference
Between the butterfly and the moth?
I like to think I'm on both sides
Eating nectar from the flowers
Chewing on someone's gray sweater
Retreating to a dark cocoon
But drawn in between times
To the light.
Everything pretty has an ugly side
Every wing's flutter would tickle
should it brush upon my cheek
And the cats, all three
Couldn't care less whether
They chase a moth or a monarch
So they're both the same to me
Sometimes I'd like to be one
More than the other
Especially when it rains
and it weighs, oh how
It weighs on me
Until my wings are moon bright
In the light
Day
Or
Night.

Sarah Thursday

Love Letter No.1: To My Pit-Bull Self

I love the teeth of your love
how you pit-bull deep
into the flesh of loving
How you make shrines
in the empty spaces,
abandoned apartments
Shrines to former residents
of borrowed books and toiletries
envelopes full of photographs
and letters in pen
How you never fill
the same space with new
but keep building out
expand the frames and floors
How you know when to change the locks
and when to nail it shut

I love how you calculate
estimate the risk
How you trust
the unnamed algorithm
the intuitive push, flashing "Yes,
love this one, let that one in!"
How soft your wrought-iron grip
holds every name tight
each face, its own story
each moment, a glass in your pane
How you refuse to argue
about the wrong
or right way to love
➤

I love how so much of it matters
how you will forgive
as many times
as they will call
and ask for it
How you defend this weakness
with the expense of wasted time
Your time-to-give being
your love currency
not words, not gifts,
not your doing-for-me
But your minutes and hours
your speak to me, eat with me
your listen and watch with me
sit in this space of air
I breathe with me is love

I love how love-greedy you get
How you collect time
and stuff it in bags and boxes
shove it on shelves, in closets
covering walls, blocking doorways
in empty apartments
You guard-dog this house
an unapologetic hoarder
How you refuse to purge it
refuse to loosen your grip
Set shrines in windowsills
light blood candles
There is always room
for more

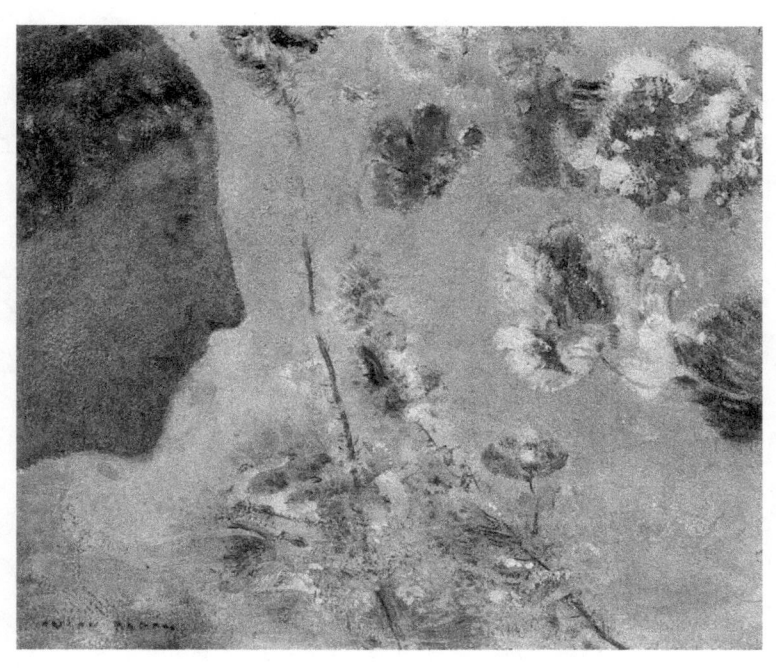

A. Garnett Weiss

In the third person

Her sharp reflection
in a mirror framed with vines.
She stares at her face,
the mask that hides what she knows:
Under lips, that smile—her skull.

What am I? she asks.
Bones, flesh, gray matter, veins, blood?
A prison of cells?
Her body confines, defines
her essence: When she lives, dies.

She, shackled and bound,
rejects her physical self,
seeks freedom elsewhere.
Spirit, soul play in her mind
where cell walls wait to be breached.

Denise R. Weuve

Pieces Make the Whole

None of my parts are original,
one of my kidneys
belongs to a 35 year-old Hispanic woman
whose name I will never know
nor how she died.
Maybe a traffic accident,
or a lover waiting beneath
her bed next to dust bunnies
and regrets forging their way
into bullets with gunpowder and tomorrows.
The other kidneys I leave where they were
except I turn them to face each other,
sad formaldehyde guinea pigs
commiserating about a life they never got to live.

My eyes stolen from a father
that disappears at seven
in the evening.
These sapphire eyes
wander truck driver style
searching for the next rest stop
or diner to forget there is a daughter
358 miles away.

The liver I have moved
to the center of my chest,
it ferments in vodka
becomes sauerkraut strong,
like the grandfather
whose hate sat so long
it had to swing from a basement beam
on a Thursday night.

➤

My heart rest where the spleen once was,
enlarged, filled with a bacteria strain
whose origin puzzles even the devil,
as he puffs on filtered Marlboro,
talks of his yesterdays
with Gabriel and Michael:
Back then, they decided what parts belonged to whom
placed crystal vocal cords into humans
so we could praise our creators.
Once we all loved.

LIZ WORTH

Suburban wilds: a self-portrait

Ocean above the cheekbones and a savage lung, the breath of devastation to match the only scar I can still see from in here.

I dream in the robes of a witch, my mouth ravaged by an April birth and temper as deep as a wolf's
but my hair speaks only of suburban wilds gone rough.
 In my hand, the spider of insomnia as swollen as an under-slept eye.

Chipped tooth from spilling out onto the street a gasping reminder of my catchall phrase: *I'm fine / I'm fine / I'm fine.*

At the wrist, ribbons of time – the dead honored in gold above flattened veins.

Skirt parted to reveal myself as the kind of girl who lets strange men's legs rest against hers on a crowded subway.

(Lift. Just a little more.)

I don't run with anyone because I don't need to.

My mind isn't as vulnerable as it used to be but
if you look me in the eye
you'll find the photograph I will become:
a socket of poetry, its tunnel
as terrible as the Moon and
burning wild.

Downcast superstition behind the earlobe, pooling in the collarbone.
Paranoia's an oil seeping from my pores,
blackheads behind bangs and drugstore concealer.
I scratch, shortened nails, a dictation of unease.

Lips, perilous. Wanting. My gaze, high.

Higher. Looking forward. Away, to something better.

Birgit Zartl

In My Head

There is a poem in my head
and dreams about a tornado
a cloud in the shape of a wedding cake
frilly and white.

But I am different.

NOTES FROM THE POETS

IVAN ARGÜELLES: I once said I read everything I write and I write everything I read. I believe that inspiration is the one true process involved in the act of creating a poem, if that's what you want to call it. I am a devotee of the Muse—she pulls me by the hair and makes me do it. No inhibitions. All worlds open, the galaxies are free fall, I embrace the cosmos as both chaotic and divine.

SUVOJIT BANERJEE: My creative process is mainly based upon observations and then me trying to put those random, haphazard things into orderly lines of words and meaningful sentences. Living in a cosmopolitan city has its certain benefits, as through my daily commotion to work and back, I can safely notice many individuals busy in their own chores. My work, from time to time, also gets influenced by other writers and their amazing works.

ALAN BIRKELBACH: My creative process is not seasonal, driven by exhaustion, coffee, or other writers. Sometimes deadlines make it happen faster. It's as much a part of the spent hours of my life as eating tacos and drinking beer and watching old movies. It doesn't depend on the Muses. My creative process is a river. I don't know the headwaters. I don't need to know.

ERIC BURKE: "Self-Portrait" was first published in *PoetsArtists* and has subsequently been remixed into a whimsical poetry video by Paul Broderick for *The Poetry Storehouse*.

MARY-MARCIA CASOLY: Blind in one eye since birth, some people find it unsettling; then again, people found this self-portrait unsettling—and so I began to muse once again, settling the subject for myself.

BETH COPELAND: "Witch" is a mirror poem. The first three stanzas establish the self-portrait of a young woman (me) imagining what she will look like when she's old. The fourth stanza, "Mirror, mirror," separates the future from the past and also functions like a hinge on a compact mirror. Stanzas 5-7 are reflections, with the lines of stanzas 1-3 written backward. Finally, we return to the young, "apple-cheeked" woman we saw at the beginning of the poem. The reference to an apple is an allusion to the witch who gave Snow White a poison apple and also looked in the mirror and asked, "Mirror, mirror on the wall. Who's the fairest of them all?"

TASHA COTTER: My process involves taking a lot of notes: I've always been an observer. I like to listen in. I like to people watch. And I like to learn a little bit about everything: in school it was torture trying to choose one subject to major in when everything was so fascinating. I take my notes (excerpts, anecdotes, quotes, found words, original ideas, bits of conversation, headlines, etc.) and begin trying to construct something like poetry. I try to root my poems in the natural world, and sometimes I'm more focused on communicating an idea, or an experience. Either way, I look for new ways *into* the world of every poem. I want to see an idea from a fresh angle, I want to listen in on the poem itself and make the music fluid, or, if necessary, pack a punch.

ADELLE FOLEY: This haiku—like most of my haiku—was scrawled in the margin of my daily newspaper as I walked to my job.

JACK FOLEY: In "Selfie," the passage in Middle English is an adaptation of a passage by John Skelton in praise of Geoffrey Chaucer. Other phrases are taken from Christopher Bernard's review of my book, EYES. The fractured passage at the conclusion of the poem is taken from my sequence, "Letters"—dedicated to the sixth Marx Brother, Typo.

ELIZABETH JACOBSON: "Girl" appears in my poetry collection, *Her Knees Pulled In* (Tres Chicas Books, 2012).

MATHIAS JANSSON" "Selfie" is an erasure poem created from the first page of *The Trial* by Franz Kafka (Penguin Classics, 2000). The poem is mixed with a self-portrait created with an on-line word-cloud tool. *The Trial* is a very important book for me and has inspired my authorship in many ways—and the first page also contains many words and lines that could be used to describe me as person.

KASEY JOHNSON: I write because something inside tells me I must, something that is often impractical and unwieldy; however, writing provides its own elixir and I always feel more alive for the effort of putting words and phrases together.

ANGELA LA VOIE: Often, I begin a poem with a line or an image that's been following me. I proceed from that impulse until I find what the poem is about it. Then I create a shape, find the rhythm, remove the clutter. After that, I allow some time to find what's missing and build texture.

STEPHEN LINSTEADT: To fully engage in the creative process requires a complete surrender to thinking about it. One's muse finds you in the space that lies between judging and criticizing yourself based on self-imposed standards. Creativity is a connection to the heart, which has a separate language from our mind's thinking and judging.

TAMARA MADISON: I like to write so much that poetry just sort of oozes out of me, even if it makes a poetic mess.

ADRIAN MANNING: "An Acceptance, A Forgiveness" was written upon the reflection of myself seen literally in the reflection of the mirror now as compared to when I was younger.

MICHAEL MARK: This poem originally appeared in the *San Diego Poetry Annual: The Best Poems of San Diego 2014*.

BOB MCNEIL: I compose poetic stun guns and tasers, weapons for the downtrodden in their battle against the opprobrious. My work is dedicated to one cause—justice.

KARLA K. MORTON: I wake every morning excited about the possibilities; wondering what miracle will reveal itself throughout the day. *Always* there is something—a glimpse of lizard changing from black to emerald; a research pearl; a poem that gets stuck in my head. It's the blessing of being able to do what you love—the excitement of a blank sheet of paper; words pulled down from the sky.

ROBERT OKAJI: One word, followed by another. Revise. Rest. Read.

ALAN PASSMAN: Some people subscribe to the idea that you should free write everyday until something sticks. Others are all about waiting for the muse to whisper in their ears. I find myself somewhere in-between. Sometimes a line or an image will pop into my head and I'll try to capture it. Then there are the moments were I doodle pictures, mostly of The Simpsons or the Ninja Turtles, and scribble lines out of boredom during professional enrichment meetings that we educators have to endure a couple times a semester. But with a poem like this that has a prompt and a project attached to it, the strictures and limitations actually aid you in that they force you to have a clear idea of what you're trying to craft with each line, each stanza, until you have something to write home about.

PAUL SANDS: "painted into a corner" was written whilst seeing an ugly reflection in the glass of a fast food eatery and old eyes staring back from a rearview mirror.

JACQUE STUKOWSKI: "Mirror oh dear mirror" is based in what I see reflected in a broken mirror.

SARAH THURSDAY: I would consider "Love Letter No. 1: To My Pit-Bull Self" a self-portrait because it describes what I love about the way that I love. This was inspired by another poet's love letter to herself. I thought about how hard it is for me to let go of others, but that I love that about myself. I love like a pit-bull.

A. GARNETT WEISS: During more than two years, I created a line-a-day for an online poetry project, posted on jcsulzenko.com. "In the third person," which first appeared there, uses the syllable count of the *tanka* form to create a portrait, deliberately written in the third person to distance the piece from the poet.

DENISE R. WEUVE: This poem is the only self-portrait I have ever written (though aren't all poems an unconscious effort to reveal self), and it is a self-portrait in organs.

LIZ WORTH: For me, creating usually involves coffee no matter what time of day it is. Occasionally it also happens with dark chocolate or banana bread, which I believe help improve concentration, or at least boost my overall levels of happiness. I always carry a notebook around and most of my writing starts with just one word or a fragment of an idea: an image, a phrase, a strange pairing of words. I take it from there and just let the writing tell me what it wants to do.

BIRGIT ZARTL: The words came during the process of falling asleep as well as while creating images to accompany the poem.

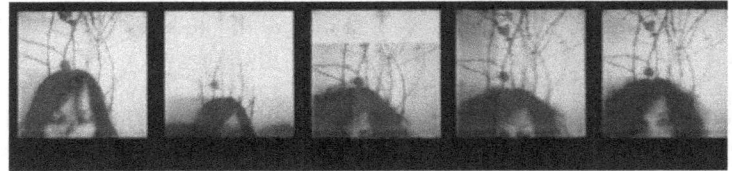

ABOUT THE POETS

KATHRYN ALMY's poetry and creative non-fiction have been published in several print and on-line publications, including the *Great Lakes Review* narrative map, *City of the Big Shoulders: An Anthology of Chicago Poetry*, *Shady Side Review*, and *The Smoking Poet*. She lives in Kalamazoo, Michigan, a town of many fine writers. Just one of these is Diane Seuss, for whose class she wrote this poem.

CYNTHIA ANDERSON lives in the high desert near Joshua Tree National Park. Her poetry books include *In the Mojave*, *Shared Visions*, and *Shared Visions II*. She is coeditor of the anthology *A Bird Black As the Sun: California Poets on Crows & Ravens*.

IVAN ARGÜELLES is a much-published innovative poet. Frequently classified as a surrealist, his poetry overreaches that definition and indeed he has pushed the envelope to epic proportions. A classicist by education, he continues exploring the so-called classical world, be it that of the Greco/Romans or that of India, in his constant experimentation with myth. Among his many books of poetry are: *What Goddess*; *Madonna Septet* (2 vols.); *Comedy, Divine, The*; *The Death of Stalin*; and *Ars Poetica*. He is currently working on a long series, *Orphic Cantos*. A Mexican-American, raised on both sides of the border, he is the identical twin of New Age prophet José Arguiles. A retired librarian, he resides in Berkeley, California.

RONALD BAATZ lives in Troy, New York with his wife Andra and their cat Mooche. His last book, *Bird Standing*, was published by Blind Dog Press in Australia.

SUVOJIT BANERJEE currently based in Kolkata, India, is stuck between the close-knit cultures of the suburbs where he grew up, and the free-swaying, liberal chores of the city, He tries to find solace, seeking the soul he has lost somewhere in the middle. His work reflects those searching-for-answers moments, and changes that he sees his city go through every single day. His work has been previously published in online magazines. He is currently working in a software company, but writes his heart out at every chance he gets.

CAROL BERG's poems are forthcoming or in *The Journal*, *Spillway*, *Sou'wester*, *Redactions*, *Pebble Lake Review*, *Fifth Wednesday Journal*, and *Verse Wisconsin*. Her most recent chapbook, *Her Vena Amoris*, is available from Red Bird Chapbooks.

ALAN BIRKELBACH's work has appeared in journals and anthologies such as *Grasslands Review*, *Borderlands*, *The Langdon Review*, and *Concho*

River Review. He is member of The Texas Institute of Letters and The Academy of American Poets. He has nine collections of poetry.

ERIC BURKE lives in Columbus, Ohio. He has an MA in Classics from The Ohio State University, but has worked as a computer programmer for the past fifteen years. More of his poems can be found in *Thrush Poetry Journal, bluestem, PANK, qarrtsiluni, Escape Into Life, decomP, A cappella Zoo, Weave Magazine* and *A Clean, Well-Lighted Place*. You can keep up with him at anomalocrinus.blogspot.com.

ANA MARIA CABALLERO has worked in finance, journalism, wine importation, and even for the Colombian government before recently becoming a mom. Now she focuses her efforts on writing poetry and book thoughts, available at thedrugstorenotebook.com. Her work has appeared in *Big River Poetry Review, Elephant Journal, East Coast Ink, Really Systems, Aviary Review, CutBank, Ghost House Review, Dagda Publishing, Toasted Cheese Literary Journal, Boston Poetry Magazine*, as well as other publications, and is forthcoming in *Pea River Review* and *Smoking Glue Gun*. She also writes a weekly poetry post for Zeteo Journal's "Zeteo is Reading" section. She lives in Colombia.

MARY-MARCIA CASOLY is the author of *Run to Tenderness* (Pantograph & Goldfish Press, 2002) and the editor of *Fresh Hot Bread*–a local zine of Waverley Writers, an open poetry forum based in the San Francisco Bay area. Her chapbook *Lost Pages of Bird Lore* was published by Small Change Series, Word Temple Press (2011). Her chapbook *Australia Dreaming* is included in the *The Ahadada Reader 3* (Ahadada Press, 2010) and is also included in *Obsession: Sestinas for the Twenty-First Century*, edited by Carolyn Beard Whitlow and Marilyn Krysl (*Dartmouth College Press*, 2014). Her poems "Song of Mayhem" and "Venus on the Half Year" were published by Silver Birch Press.

TOBI COGSWELL is a multiple Pushcart nominee and a Best of the Net nominee. Credits include or are forthcoming in various journals in the U.S., UK., Sweden, and Australia. In 2012 and 2013, she was short-listed for the Fermoy International Poetry Festival. In 2013, she received Honorable Mention for the Rachel Sherwood Poetry Prize. Her sixth and latest chapbook is *Lapses & Absences* (Blue Horse Press). She is the co-editor of San Pedro River Review (sprreview.com).

BETH COPELAND lived in Japan, India, and North Carolina as a child. Her book *Traveling Through Glass* received the 1999 Bright Hill Press Poetry Book Award, and her second poetry collection *Transcendental Telemarketer* was released by BlazeVOX books in 2012. Her poems have been widely published in literary journals and have received awards from *Atlanta Review, North American Review, The North Carolina*

Poetry Society, and *Peregrine*. Two of her poems have been nominated for a Pushcart Prize. She is an English instructor at Methodist University in Fayetteville, North Carolina. She lives in a log cabin in the country with her husband, Phil Rech.

ANTHONY COSTELLO'S poetry has appeared in magazines and journals in America, Australia, Austria, France, Scotland, Ireland, and England. *The Mask*, his first collection of poems, was published in October 2014 by Lapwing Publications, Belfast.

TASHA COTTER'S first full-length collection, *Some Churches*, was released in 2013 with Gold Wake Press. Her work has appeared in or is forthcoming in *NANO Fiction*, *Verse Daily*, and *Contrary Magazine*. She lives in Lexington, Kentucky, where she is at work on a novel.

KAILA DAVIS is a student at Marcus Garvey Academy in Detroit, Michigan.

DANIEL PATRICK DELANEY recently completed a memoir entitled *Mary's Last*. He lives and writes in a suburb of Philadelphia.

Rodrigo V. Dela Peña, Jr. has been a fellow for various writers' workshops in the Philippines. His poems have been published in the *Quarterly Literary Review Singapore*, *Kartika Review: An Asian American Literary Arts Journal*, *Corpus: Journal of the Los Angeles AIDS Project*, *The Guardian* (UK), and other journals and anthologies. He works as a marketing communications specialist in Singapore.

DAVID DIAZ is a twenty-six-year-old bike tech and part-time editor at *American Mustard* who lives in Lakewood, California. He received his B.A. in Literature and Creative Writing from Cal State Long Beach, and is currently pursuing his MFA there. His work has been featured by Cadence Collective, Birds Thumb, and has a chapbook titled *Loogie Papers* that was published by Tiny Splendor Press in 2012. David loves concerts, poetry readings, book releases, drive-in movies, and he is addicted to Los Angeles.

BARBARA EKNOIAN'S work has appeared in *Pearl*, *Chiron Review*, *RE)VERB* and Silver Birch Press's *Silver*, *Green*, and *Summer* anthologies. She has received two Pushcart Prize nominations and is a longtime member of Donna Hilbert's poetry workshop in Long Beach, California. Her fiction was featured in the 2009 Sixth Annual Emerging Voices Show produced by Sally Shore's New Short Fiction Series. Her first young adult novel, *Chances Are: A Jersey Girl Comes of Age*, and her poetry book, *Why I Miss New Jersey*, are available at Amazon. She's currently writing a generational novel.

ADELLE FOLEY is a retirement administrator, an arts activist, and a writer of haiku. Her column, "High Street Neighborhood News," appears monthly in *The MacArthur Metro*. Her poems have appeared in various magazines, in textbooks, and in Columbia University Press's Internet database, the *Columbia Granger's World of Poetry*. Along the Bloodline is her first book-length collection. Beat poet Michael McClure writes, "Adelle Foley's haikus show us humanity. Their vitality and imagination shine from her compassion; from seeing things as they truly are." Visit her at jack-adellefoley.com.

JACK FOLEY is a widely published, innovative California poet. He has published thirteen books of poetry, five books of criticism, and *Visions and Affiliations*, a chronoencyclopedia of California poetry from 1940-2005. His radio show, *Cover to Cover*, is heard on Berkeley, California, radio station KPFA every Wednesday at three p.m., and his column, "Foley's Books," appears in the online magazine *Alsop Review*. In 2010, the Berkley Poetry Festival recognized Foley with its Lifetime Achievement Award, and June 5, 2010 was proclaimed "Jack Foley Day" in Berkeley. With poet Clara Hsu, Foley is publisher of Poetry Hotel Press. Foley's recent publications include *EYES: Selected Poems* (Poetry Hotel Press) and *LIFE*, a chapbook (Word Palace Press). With his wife Adelle, Foley performs his work (often "multi-voiced" pieces) frequently in the San Francisco Bay Area. Their performances can be found on YouTube.

MICHAEL FRIEDMAN is a student in the MFA in Creative Writing program at Queens University at Charlotte. He lives with his lovely wife and two bat-shit crazy dogs near Chapel Hill, North Carolina. To help pay the bills, he works as a medical writer, preparing drug regulatory and scientific documents. His poems have appeared (or are slated to appear) in *Golden Walkman Magazine*, *Camel Saloon*, *Eunoia Review*, and *Stray Branch*.

JEANNINE HALL GAILEY recently served as Redmond, Washington's second Poet Laureate. She is the author of four books of poetry: *Becoming the Villainess*, *She Returns to the Floating World*, *Unexplained Fevers*, and, upcoming in 2015 from Mayapple Press, *The Robot Scientist's Daughter*. Her web site is www. webbish6.com.

PHILLIP GIAMBRI, aka "The Ancient Mariner," is a product of the streets of South Philadelphia. He obtained his deviant perspective on life listening to Jean Shepherd on WOR radio back in the '50s. Fleeing Philly at seventeen, he served in the military, has been an actor, hairstylist, stoner, janitor, writer, drifter, recording engineer, hired hand, poet, traveling salesman, barfly, banker, biker, bronco buster, announcer, mail-order minister, photographer, and "Computer Guru." He arrived in New York City in '68, joined the hippie pilgrimage to

St. Marks Place, and never left. He's attended too many schools to mention, studying nearly everything, without ever attaining a degree in anything. He produces and hosts a popular monthly spoken word/poetry event, *Rimes of The Ancient Mariner*, as well as special collaborative events with other artist/performers—most recently the very successful, Barflies & Broken Angels. His website Ancient Mariner Tales offers bored web surfers a glimpse into his futile search for self-discovery and meaning. He can be found in downtown NYC, regularly spinning yarns and telling tall tales anywhere that will tolerate him.

JOHN A. GROCHALSKI is the author of *The Noose Doesn't Get Any Looser After You Punch Out* (Six Gallery Press 2008), *Glass City* (Low Ghost Press, 2010), *In The Year of Everything Dying* (Camel Saloon, 2012), *Starting with the Last Name Grochalski* (Coleridge Street Books, 2014), and the novel, *The Librarian* (Six Gallery Press, 2013). Grochalski currently lives in Brooklyn, New York, where he constantly worries about the high cost of everything.

CLARA HSU practices the art of multidimensional being: mother, musician, purveyor of Clarion Music Center (1982-2005), traveler, translator, and poet. Since 2009, she has co-hosted with John Rhodes the monthly San Francisco Open Mic Poetry Podcast TV Show. In 2013, she cofounded Poetry Hotel Press with Jack Foley. Clara has been published internationally. Her book of poetry *The First to Escape* was released in July 2014.

ELIZABETH JACOBSON is the author of the poetry collection, *Her Knees Pulled In* (Tres Chicas Books, 2012). She is the founding director of the WingSpanPoetry Project, which brings weekly poetry classes to the residents at the Esperanza Shelter for Battered Families in Santa Fe, New Mexico, and creates poetry workshops for various programs at other local shelters. She has taught writing for over twenty-five years at colleges and elementary schools, in both New York and New Mexico, most recently with ArtWorks in Santa Fe. Elizabeth is the winner of the 2013 Mountain West Writer's Contest from Western Humanities Review, the recipient of the Jim Sagel Prize for poetry from Puerto del Sol, and she has an MFA from Columbia University.

LOUKIA M. JANAVARAS, originally from Minneapolis, Minnesota, lived in Athens, Greece, for eleven years, and currently lives in Abu Dhabi, United Arab Emirates. In 2010, she received an Honorable Mention in the Writer's Digest 79th Annual Writing Competition for *The Neighbor* in the Memoirs/Personal Essay category. In 2012, her work appeared in several publications including *The Creative Writer, Gloom Cupboard, Wilderness House Literary Review, Turbulence, The Newtowner,*

Pyrta, Riverbabble, Decades Review, Torrid Literature Journal, Down in the Dirt, Eskimo Pie, Shadow Road Quarterly, and *Eunoia Review.*

MATHIAS JANSSON is a Swedish art critic and poet. He has contributed with visual and experimental poetry to magazines such as *Lex-ICON, Eremonaut, Anatematiskpress, Quarter After #4,* and *Maintenant 8: A Journal of Contemporary Dada.* He has also published a chapbook at "this is visual poetry" and contributed with poetry to anthologies from Silver Birch Press. Visit him at mathiasjansson72.blogspot.se.

JAX NTP holds an MFA in Poetry from California State University, Long Beach. Jax was the former editor-in-chief of *RipRap Literary Journal,* and is the current associate editor of *The Fat City Review.* Jax has an affinity for jellyfish and polaris and a fetish for miniature succulent terrariums. Visit her at jaxntppoet.tumblr.com.

KASEY JOHNSON received a BA in English from Reed College and an MA in English Literature from the University of New Mexico. She works for a healthcare nonprofit in Seattle, Washington, and is an editorial assistant and book review editor for *CALYX, A Journal of Art and Literature by Women.* Her work is forthcoming in *Corium Magazine, Prick of the Spinkle,* and *Verdad.*

JENNIFER LYNN KROHN was born and raised in Albuquerque, New Mexico, where she currently lives with her husband. She earned her MFA from the University of New Mexico, and she currently teaches English at Central New Mexico Community College and Santa Fe University of Art and Design. Jennifer has published work in The *Saranac Review, Río Grande Review, Prick of the Spindle, In the Garden of the Crow, Versus Literary Journal,* and *Gingerbread Literary Magazine.*

ANGELA LA VOIE is a former journalist, whose stories have been published in *The Chicago Sun-Times, Detroit Free Press, The Dallas Morning News,* on MSNBC.com, and elsewhere. She is an MFA candidate in creative nonfiction and poetry at Antioch University Los Angeles. Recent essays have appeared in *Skirt!* magazine and *Catharsis Journal.*

ROZ LEVINE is a Los Angeles poet who has written poems since the age of eight. When she retired several years ago, writing became her number-one passion. Words have helped her navigate cancer and helped her maintain her sanity in a not-so-sane world. Her work has been published in various venues, including *On The Bus, Forever in Love, Deliver Me, The Sun, Pulse, Cultural Weekly,* and *Poetry Superhighway.*

ALEXANDER LIMAREV is a freelance artist, mail art artist, curator, and poet from Russia. Participated in more than two hundred and fifty international projects and exhibitions. His artwork is part of private and museum collections of forty-five countries. His art and poetry have been featured in various online publications including *Time for a Vispo, Expoesia Visual Experimental, The New Post-Literate: A Gallery of Asemic Writing, Baa:Be:l, Nothing and Insight, Foffof, Spontaneous Combustion Language Image Lab, Fooom, Poezine, Degu: A Journal of Signs, Existere, ffoOom, Chernovik, The White Raven, Undergroundbooks.org, ÖÖŏŏŏ, Boek861, Tip of the Knife, Bukowski on Wry, Kiosko (libera, skeptika, transkultura), Microlit, Metazen, Blackbird, Zoomoozophone Review,* and *M58.*

STEPHEN LINSTEADT is a painter, poet, and writer. He is the author of the book *Scalar Heart Connection,* which is concerned with humanity's connection, or lack thereof, with Nature, the Earth, and the global community. He has published articles about metaphysics and consciousness in *Whole Life Times, Creations Magazine,* and others. His poetry is published in *Moments of the Soul* (Spirit First), *Solstice, Cradle Songs* (Quill and Parchment Press), *Saint Julian Press, Poets on Site, Pirene's Fountain,* and others. His paintings have appeared in *Reed Magazine, Badlands Literary Journal,* and *Birmingham Arts Journal* and can be seen at StephenLinsteadtStudio.com.

TAMARA MADISON teaches English and French at a public high school in Los Angeles. Raised on a citrus farm in the California desert, Tamara's life has taken her many places, including Europe and the former Soviet Union, where she spent fifteen months in the 1970s. A swimmer and dog lover, Tamara says, "All I ever wanted to do with my life was write, and I mostly write poetry because it suits my lifestyle. I like the way one can say so much in the economical space of a poem."

ADRIAN MANNING hails from Leicester, England, where he writes poems and is editor of Concrete Meat Press (concretemeatpress.co.uk).

MICHAEL MARK is a hospice volunteer and long distance walker—his latest journey was the Camino De Santiago. His poetry has appeared in *Angle Journal, Awakening Consciousness Magazine, Empty Mirror, Everyday Poets, Forge Journal, OutsideIn Magazine, Petrichor Review, San Diego Poetry Annual Scapegoat Journal, Spillway, Red Booth Review, Red Paint Hill, Sleet Magazine, The Thing of it, The New York Times,* UPAYA, *Word Soup End Hunger,* and other nice places. He thanks you for looking at his profile, though this isn't him.

DANIEL MCGINN's work has appeared numerous anthologies and publications. His full-length collection of poems, *1000 Black Umbrellas,* was released by Write Bloody Press. He recently earned an MFA in writing from Vermont College of Fine Arts. He and his wife, poet Lori McGinn, are natives of Southern California. They have three children, six grandchildren, two parakeets, and a very good dog.

VICTORIA MCGRATH is an emerging poet who lives in country NSW, Australia, and is a graduate of the Australian National University. She has won a number of poetry awards and was shortlisted in 2013 for the prestigious Newcastle Poetry Prize. She has been published in journals and anthologies in Australia and the US and has performed in a range of events, including twice as featured poet at the Bundanoon Winterfest. A publisher has expressed interest in her first, not quite finished, manuscript.

BOB MCNEIL was influenced by the Beats and the Dadaists. Furthermore, even after all these years of being a professional illustrator, spoken word artist, and writer, he still hopes to express and address the needs of the human mosaic.

ANN MENEBROKER never wrote a poem in her place of birth, Washington D.C. She continues to write them in her California environment, however. Putting aside the usual, where she's been published, how many books, all of that, she prefers to say that on June 22, 2014, she read with three wonderful long-time Sacramento friends, to a full house, and with a grateful heart. The reading was introduced as "Tough Old Broads Poetry."

DANIELLE MITCHELL is one of ten emerging poets featured in *Pop Art: An Anthology of Southern California Poetry* (Moon Tide Press). Her prose poems have appeared in journals such as *Connotation Press, decomP, Union Station Magazine, Cease, Cows & Freeze Ray*. Danielle directs The Poetry Lab in Long Beach, California, where she hosts workshops & craft seminars. She is an alumna of the Squaw Valley Community of Writers & holds degrees in Women's Studies & Creative Writing from the University of Redlands. She currently guest writes for DIY MFA & blogs at poetryofdanielle.com.

KARLA K. MORTON, the 2010 Texas Poet Laureate, is a Councilor of the Texas Institute of Letters and a graduate of Texas A&M University. Described as "one of the most adventurous voices in American poetry," she is a Betsy Colquitt Award Winner, twice an Indie National Book Award Winner, the recipient of the Writer-in-Residency E2C Grant, and the author of nine collections of poetry. Morton has been nominated for the Pushcart Prize, is a nominee for the National Cowgirl Hall of Fame, and established an ekphrastic collaborative touring exhibit titled: *No End of Vision: Texas as Seen By Two Laureates*, pairing photography with poetry with Texas Poet Laureate Alan Birkelbach. Morton's work has been used by many students in their UIL Contemporary Poetry contests, and was recently featured with seven other prominent authors in *8 Voices: Contemporary Poetry of the American*

Southwest. Her forthcoming book (her tenth), *Constant State of Leaping* (The Texas Review Press), arrives Fall 2014.

ROBERT OKAJI'S work has appeared in *Boston Review*, *Otoliths*, *Prime Number Magazine*, *Clade Song*, and *Vayavya*, among others. He lives in Texas with his wife and two dogs.

JAY PASSER's work has been published in print and online since 1988. He is the author of numerous chapbooks, the most recent being *At the End of the Street* (corrupt press, 2012).

ALAN PASSMAN is a man who strives for impossibility. His aesthetic is one that blends blatant pop cultural nerdery with red-hot, American male deviancy. He's been published in *Crack the Spine*, *Carnival*, *Bank Heavy Press*, and, coming this fall, he will be featured in *Multiverse: An Anthology of Superhero Poetry of Superhuman Proportions* from Write Bloody Publishing. He received his BA and MFA from California State University, Long Beach, for Creative Writing and Poetry respectively. Currently, he teaches English at Long Beach City College.

D.A. (DAVID) PRATT lives in Regina, Saskatchewan, Canada. In 2013, his short prose piece "Encountering Bukowski—Some Canadian Notes" appeared in the Silver Birch Press *Bukowski Anthology*.

BILLY ROBERSON is a student at Marcus Garvey Academy in Detroit, Michigan.

RIZWAN SALEEM is a banker by profession residing in Dubai, United Arab Emirates, and fancies himself a poet of the lowest caliber. The thoughts and expressions detailed in his works are of his various escapades suffered through life and of the profound surprise of having survived long enough to pen them into words. The writer wishes that readers may be able to offer a sardonic smile upon reading his work and relate themselves to his rhymes.

PAUL SANDS was born in 1962 and was raised close to the River Trent in Nottingham, U.K. He attended comprehensive school in Selston and worked from the age of 16 in the IT industry, between playing in noisy beat combos, for twenty-seven years until downsized and outsourced in 2006. After dallying with photography, he now lives and attempts to work in Lincolnshire. He self-published his first collection of poetry, *Ego...Ergo*, in June 2012. The summer of 2013 saw him publish a second collection entitled *Scratch*.

REBECCA SCHUMEJDA is the author of *Waiting at the Dead End Diner* (Bottom Dog Press, 2014), *Cadillac Men* (NYQ Books, 2012), *Falling Forward* (sunnyoutside, 2009), and several chapbooks. She received her MA from San Francisco State University. She lives with her family in New York's Hudson Valley. Visit her at rebeccaschumejda.com.

ROY ANTHONY SHABLA is a painter and poet who lives in the Los Angeles area. He was just appointed the director of collections for the Downey Museum of Art. He currently has thirteen books in print. "I am the king of the world" is an excerpt from a longer, deconstructed poem that incorporates several languages. It is an important part of the sound art performance piece, *babbel*, which was first performed at Stay Gallery, January 2014.

SHEIKHA A. currently lives in Karachi, Pakistan, after moving from the United Arab Emirates, and believes the transition has definitely stimulated a different tunnel of thought. With publication credits in magazines such as *Red Fez*, *American Diversity Report*, *Open Road Review*, *Mad Swirl*, *Danse Macabre du Jour*, *Rose Red Review*, *The Penmen Review*, and several anthologies, she has also authored a poetry collection entitled *Spaced* (Hammer and Anvil Books), available on Kindle, and edits poetry for *eFiction India*. Visit her blog at sheikha82.wordpress.com.

JAKIA SMITH is a student at Marcus Garvey Academy in Detroit, Michigan.

KIMBERLY SMITH is a student at Marcus Garvey Academy in Detroit, Michigan.

EDDIE STEWART is a student at Marcus Garvey Academy in Detroit, Michigan.

JACQUE STUKOWSKI hails from Chicago, Illinois. She works as a full-time graphic designer, but writing, music, and photography are her passions. Jacque's blog God[isms] features her personal stories of life as Christian woman with BP and ADHD. She's found therapy through sharing her creative gifts of design, writing poetry, and taking photos that capture various topics. She often uses metaphors and symbolism to connect the reader with real-life things in nature to convey the message she's writing about. Jacque is currently working on her first novel, and her photography is frequently featured at Broken Light Collective.com.

ROSE SWARTZ is a writer and visual artist from Kalamazoo, Michigan. She currently lives in Portland, Oregon, where she practices darkroom photography and creative writing. She travels frequently. She's been a poetry editor for Hayden's Ferry Review and Asylum Lake Magazine. Her writing has most recently appeared in *Carnival Magazine*, *Really System Magazine*, and *Coal Hill Review*. Her chapbook, *All Along the California Coast*, came out this year on Diamond Wave Press (diamondwavepress.com). Photos from her photography-project-in-progress, a two-week cross-country trip via back roads, can be viewed at rosa.swartz.tumblr.com.

SIMEN MOFLAG TALLERAAS is a Norwegian citizen, born in the '90s. He's fond of found poetry, surrealist imagery, and all forms of experimental poetic literature. Several Norwegian newspapers have published his socially conscious poetry.

KEYNA THOMAS is a freelance writer of poetry and short stories, as well as a part-time administrative assistant at a state university, where she is working on her Bachelor's. She has worked in New England as a reporter and staff writer for MediaNews Group. There, she learned that true stories about people are almost always as interesting as fiction. Since then, she has been writing a short novel that merges the two. Keyna grew up in Central Massachusetts, where she now lives and works. She and some of her 140-character (or less) ramblings can be found at twitter.com/Keyna.

SARAH THURSDAY calls Long Beach, California, her home, where she advocates for local poets and poetry events. She runs a Long-Beach-focused poetry website called CadenceCollective.net, co-hosts a monthly reading with one of her poetry heroes, G. Murray Thomas, and just started Sadie Girl Press as a summer job and way to help publish local and emerging poets. She just completed her first full-length poetry collection, *All the Tiny Anchors*. Find and follow her on sarahthursday.com, Facebook, or Twitter.

A. GARNETT WEISS, writing as JC Sulzenko, has been featured on local and national radio and television, online, and in anthologies and chapbooks. Her centos have won a number of recent awards, and various newspapers have carried her creative non-fiction. She has appeared often on behalf of the Ottawa International Writers Festival, which hosted the premiere of her play about Alzheimer's disease, *What My Grandma Means to Say*, and which also launched her sixth book for children, adapted from the play, In 2012, she served as poet mentor for The Gryphon Trio's *Listen UP! Ottawa* music and poetry composition project. She also received the Ottawa Public Library's Order of Friendship for "outstanding volunteer service."

DENISE R. WEUVE is a 2013 Pushcart Prize nominee who resides in Southern California. Her poetry has been published in numerous journals, and she has won a couple of awards here and there, like the annual Sheila-Na-Gig contest and Donald Drury Award in Writing. In the past, she has edited for various literary magazines and is currently associate poetry editor for *Cease, Cows! Her chapbook *The Truck Driver's Daughter* will be released in 2014 by ELJ Press. None of this has impressed her cat, friends, or family, who can either be found chewing up her poems, calling to do a night out, or asking when she is going to get a real job. Currently, she attends Queens University of Charlotte, where she is obtaining an MFA in Poetry.

LIZ WORTH is a Toronto-based author. Her debut book, *Treat Me Like Dirt: An Oral History of Punk in Toronto and Beyond*, was the first to give an in-depth account of Toronto's early punk scene. Liz's first poetry collection, *Amphetamine Heart*, was released in 2011, and her first novel, *PostApoc*, was released in October 2013. She has also rewritten Andy Warhol's *a: A Novel* as poetry. You can reach her at lizworth.com.

BIRGIT ZARTL is a painter and photographer, based in Vienna, Austria. Her main interest lies in subconscious symbolism and imagery.

www.ingramcontent.com/pod-product-compliance
Lightning Source LLC
Chambersburg PA
CBHW061322040426
42444CB00011B/2725